Famous

Gangsters

Al Capone and The Kray Twins

2 Books in 1

Roger Harrington

Table of Contents

Al Capone

American Gangster Stories

Roger Harrington

Humble Beginnings

Although he ultimately became notorious as a crime boss engaged in bootlegging, gambling and various other illegal activities and was named by the Chicago Crime Commission as 'Public Enemy Number 1', Al Capone's beginnings were decidedly humble.

Alphonse Gabriel Capone was born on 17th January 1899 in Brooklyn, New York City. Although many people turn to crime to escape their poor background, this wasn't really the case with Al Capone. His parents were respectable people who emigrated from Italy to Austria-Hungary (now Croatia) in 1893 and then by ship to the U.S.

Father Gabriele was employed as a barber while mother Teresa worked for some time as a seamstress. When they arrived in America, they already had two sons and Teresa was pregnant with a third child. They lived initially in a squalid tenement building near the Navy Yard, a generally rough and noisy area although the family managed to remain normal and law-abiding.

Al Capone was born the fourth of nine children, one of whom died at the age of one. Two brothers, Rafaela James (known as 'Ralph') and Salvatore (or 'Frank'), eventually joined Al in his criminal activities. Ironically, given Capone's later career, one brother — Vincenzo, who changed his name to Richard Hart — became a prohibition agent.

Unhappy Schooldays

Capone attended a strict Catholic school where he struggled with the rules and the brutality he faced there. Despite this, he was a promising pupil at least at first. This all changed, however, when he was expelled at the age of fourteen for hitting a female teacher in the face.

The boy's formal education ended at this point and his descent into a criminal career had begun. The transition was no doubt also helped by the family's move, when he was aged eleven, to Park Slope in Brooklyn. This was a much more ethnically mixed area of New York and it resulted in Capone being affected by wider cultural influences.

Included among those influences was Capone's membership of several local gangs. He initially joined the Junior Forty Thieves and then moved on to the Bowery Boys, the Brooklyn Rippers, James Street Boys Gang and eventually the powerful Five Points Gang in Lower Manhattan. The latter was run by gangster Johnny Torrio, who was to have a huge influence on Capone's life.

Early Career

After being expelled from school, Capone took on various odd jobs in the Brooklyn area, including working in a bowling alley and a candy store. Full-time work followed, primarily at the Harvard Inn on Coney Island, owned by mobster Frankie Yale, where Capone worked as a bartender and bouncer.

Whilst working there, Capone inadvertently insulted a woman patron, resulting in her brother, Frank Gallucio, slashing him across the face with a knife in retribution. This caused three prominent scars on the left side of his face that resulted in the press nicknaming him 'Scarface'. After that, Capone always tried to present the other side of his face to cameras and described his scars as 'war wounds', despite never serving in the military.

On Frankie Yale's insistence, Capone apologised to Gallucio for insulting his sister. Nevertheless, he appeared not to bear a grudge since he later hired Gallucio as his bodyguard.

Becoming a Married Man

On 30th December 1918, aged only nineteen, Capone married Irish Catholic Mae Josephine Coughlin. Since he was under 21 at the time, he required the written permission of his parents before the wedding could go ahead. The couple remained married until his death and had one child,

Albert Francis 'Sonny' Capone, who was born just prior to their marriage.

The marriage appeared to change Capone, if only temporarily, and he reportedly worked for a period as a bookkeeper. Within little more than a year, however, he was off to Chicago to work for old associate Johnny Torrio and his career as a criminal really took off.

Moving On

The reasons for Capone's move to Chicago from New York in 1920 are somewhat unclear. There is a belief that the unexpected death of his father prompted a change while there were stories that there was a need to get out after severely injuring a rival gang member. More likely is that he went at the request of Johnny Torrio, for whom he'd worked when aged only fifteen, since he immediately became employed by him on arriving there.

At the time, Torrio operated as an enforcer for crime boss James 'Big Jim' Colosimo. When Colosimo was murdered on 11th May 1920, with the culprits rumored to be either

Capone or Frankie Yale, Torrio took over the business.

Capone initially worked as a bouncer in a brothel. Here he contracted syphilis, which went untreated because the symptoms subsided and he wrongly assumed the disease had somehow been cured. It returned with a vengeance later and was to eventually lead to the deterioration in his physical and mental health that ultimately contributed to his early death.

Opportunities Abound

The start of the Prohibition era in 1920 offered great opportunities to make immense amounts of money from illegal bootlegging operations. And Chicago was ideally located to capitalize on these opportunities, being well served by railroads and with easy access to huge areas of the USA and Canada.

Added to that, Chicago was a city that had grown from a mere 30,000 people in 1850 to around three million when Capone arrived. The influx of all types and nationalities provided a ready market for what he was supplying.

Although Colosimo had been active in operating many brothels and gambling dens in the city, he had supposedly wanted nothing to do with bootlegging. Torrio, however, had no such qualms and, on taking over, went into bootlegging in a big way.

Capone's business sense led to him taking over the running of the Four Deuces, a whorehouse, speakeasy and gambling joint that was also Torrio's headquarters. The basement area was reputedly used to torture opponents and those with useful information. Capone soon became Torrio's right-hand man, helping to run the biggest organised crime group in Chicago.

Torrio had a reputation as a 'gentleman gangster' and his style was to avoid conflict with rival gangs, instead preferring to negotiate with them over territory agreements. These attempts failed in the case of Dean O'Banion, the leader of the smaller North Side Gang, whose territory was increasingly threatened by the Genna brothers and apparently with Torrio's blessing.

On Torrio's orders or agreement, O'Banion was murdered on 24th October 1924. O'Banion's close friend Hymie Weiss took over the North Side Gang and made revenge over the killing a priority. That resulted in an unsuccessful attempt on Capone's life in January 1925 and Torrio being shot multiple times twelve days later.

Capone's Ascension to Gang Boss

Although Torrio recovered from his injuries, he retired and handed over full control to Capone. He returned to his native Italy for a period of three years before eventually coming back to the US.

At the age of 26, Al Capone was in charge of an organization, which he referred to as the 'Outfit' that included gambling, prostitution and illegal breweries backed up by a transport network that spread across America and into Canada.

All of that came with protection from law enforcement agencies and politicians, together with a degree of ignorance — some newspapers describing him as a 'boxing promoter' due to him having promoted local fights in order to raise extra money. Capone marked his elevation by increasing the organization's revenue through the use of uncompromising tactics.

Any businesses that refused to deal with him were treated harshly. That generally meant their property being blown up, around one hundred people losing their lives during the 1920s to these bombings.

Capone's hardline approach meant that the power vacuum usually associated with a gang boss's demise never happened. He quickly smashed all the opposition that would otherwise have been fighting for control and established a supremacy that few dared threaten.

In the event, the outcome was a significant increase in brothels and a business that generated revenue of as much as $100 million annually, equivalent to around $1.2 billion today. Capone had in place a network of brothels and speakeasies throughout the city and controlled the sale of alcohol to more than 10,000 speakeasies. By 1929, his personal net worth had risen to over $40 million — a figure that equates to about $550 million at today's values.

Gaining Influence

In order to gain the protection of Chicago city hall for his bootlegging operations, Capone is widely believed to have helped Republican William Hale Thompson gain election as mayor. By 1923, having put up with the corruption of Thompson as well as his alliance with Torrio for eight years, Chicago elected reformer William Dever as his successor. Fearing a crackdown on his operations, Torrio decided a second base was needed and sent Capone to nearby Cicero to establish a presence there.

Building a Political Base

The potential crackdown on racketeering in Chicago brought into focus the importance of increasing protection against the law enforcement agencies. That objective was largely achieved by a combination of bribery and strong-arm tactics.

To protect their gambling dens, brothels and other illegal activities, Capone and Brothers Frank and Ralph attained leading positions in the Cicero city government. This was partly achieved by threatening voters and kidnapping the election workers of their opponents, although Frank was killed in a Chicago police shoot out during this period.

Capone used threats, bribery and violence to move existing gangster gangs aside. This caused a change in political opinion and existing mayor Joseph Klenha, who was up for re-election in April 1924, asked Capone for help. He responded by turning gang members loose on the election.

Klenha's opponent was forced out of his headquarters by gunmen, the challenger for the city clerk's office was pistol whipped and helpers and campaigners were beaten up. Election workers were kidnapped, policemen attacked and voters who were planning to support the opposition were prevented from voting.

The whole election fell into chaos and officials asked for help. As a result, seventy Chicago police officers were deputised and five squads of detectives were sent to Cicero to restore order.

One squad came across three gunmen who included Al and Frank Capone. In the shoot-out that followed, Frank was killed and Al managed to escape unharmed. In common with many such episodes over several years, he was not arrested.

The campaign of violence was effective, however, since Klenha was comfortably re-elected. With Klenha in his pocket, Capone established his headquarters in the Hawthorne Inn and took over the town.

Klenha was again elected in 1928, although this time there was no repeat of the violence due to a large Chicago police presence. By 1932, the electorate had had enough and Klenha was voted out. Capone, however, wasn't overly concerned since by this time he was already serving time for tax evasion.

Back in Chicago, in the 1927 election, Thompson won the backing of Capone, allegedly to the extent of a $250,000 contribution, by campaigning for a wide open city that might even include the re-opening of illegal saloons.

Thompson won by a narrow margin in 1927, helped by a bombing campaign on the 10th April polling day that targeted booths in areas that were thought to support Thompson's rival William Emmett Dever. Also a victim was lawyer Octavius Granadary, who challenged Thompson's candidature for the African-American vote and was shot and killed after being chased through the streets by cars containing armed men.

Capone's bomber, James Belcastro, was charged along with four police officers but all charges were subsequently dropped when witnesses retracted their statements.

Maintaining Authority and Security

For a period, Capone moved his Chicago headquarters to fifty rooms within the luxurious Metropole Hotel. This was a statement of his authority in the knowledge that Mayor Thompson would comply with his wishes. That authority extended to his mobsters carrying official police department issue cards stating that the bearer should be treated with the same courtesy as police officers.

Whilst the actions in connection with the elections served to safeguard Capone's operations, his life was still in danger. Despite this, he was generally unarmed but was always accompanied by a minimum of two bodyguards and even acquired an armor plated car for his protection. He rarely risked travelling during the day, preferring night-time travel as a safer option.

There was also a tendency to get away from Chicago at every opportunity. This often included taking a night train to various cities, booking at the last minute an entire carriage for Capone and his entourage. On arrival at their destination, they'd book into a luxury hotel under assumed names, occupying suites for up to a week.

Creating his Miami Beach Base

In 1928, Capone bought a 14-room house on Palm Island, Florida. It was purchased from beer magnate Clarence Busch for $40,000 and had ten-foot walls behind which Capone could get away from public attention.

It was a place where he could escape Chicago's harsh winters while still being able to direct operations from there, sometimes on the 32-foot cabin cruiser he had acquired. Palm Island was also the place where Capone eventually spent his final days on release from prison.

The purchase of the Florida mansion was partly prompted by a need to break free from the pressures and persecutions of Chicago. It also resulted from a journey between various cities where Capone was greeted at each one by a large police presence and it was made clear he was not welcome there.

Capone liked Florida in general and Miami in particular. This was due to the benign year round weather and the indulgent lifestyle where gambling was everywhere and prohibition was largely ignored.

Planning to establish a base there, he booked into the penthouse suite of the Ponce de Leon Hotel under the name of 'A Costa'. He also rented a house on Miami Beach for his wife and son at a cost of $2,500 per month.

The property was leased under the name of 'Al Brown' as a precaution. Nevertheless, the owners soon found out who the real occupant was and worried about the safety of the building and its contents. Their fears were misplaced because Capone actually upgraded some of the contents to meet his lifestyle needs and ensured all bills related to the property were settled in full.

How the Palm Island Property was Acquired

The Ponce de Leon Hotel was operated by Parker Henderson Junior, who was eager to please and provided favors for Capone, including purchasing a number of guns for him. He also acted as a real estate representative for Capone and helped locate and acquire the Palm Island mansion where he spent his final days.

The mansion was bought on 27th March 1928 but, knowing Capone wouldn't be welcome as a resident, Henderson signed all the papers as though he was the purchaser and owner of the property.

Capone spent $100,000 improving the estate, adding what was at the time the largest privately-owned swimming pool with a filtration system that could handle sea or fresh water. Also added were new garages, a boathouse, decking and gardens. Capone supervised all the work and insisted on the best of everything but, like the house, it was all done in Henderson's name.

To ensure the highest standards of work, Capone treated all his workers well. That included providing them with sumptuous lunches and the result was a renovation project of which he was proud.

It took some time before it was realized who the real owner of the property was. This was despite Henderson transferring the mansion into the name of Mae Capone, Al's wife.

Attempts to Move Capone Out of Florida

Economic events had slowed the property market and a hurricane in 1926 had not helped matters. So it was feared Capone's arrival would make matters worse and turn Miami Beach into a place where people didn't want to come.

Several local groups protested at Capone's presence in Miami, prompting a meeting with the mayor and the Miami Beach city mayor. They appeared satisfied with his explanation that he was there for relaxation and would not cause any trouble.

Although the area was alive with illegal gambling, prostitution and other corrupt activities, to which local officials had turned a blind eye; Capone was accused of bringing in gambling. There was a newspaper-led campaign to get him out and a move by the American League to strip him of his constitutional rights.

The Miami Beach city council tried to sue him while the governor of Florida attempted to have him arrested. This occurred on a few occasions but only resulted in him being jailed once. Constant surveillance failed to curb his activities and endless harassment did not succeed in driving him out. Capone did attempt to improve relationships by hosting a series of goodwill dinners but opinions were too firmly entrenched to change matters much.

Residents campaigned for his removal and various authorities combined with business leaders to support this action. Many of the latter, however, saw Capone's presence as a business opportunity and efforts to move him out failed.

Those attempts included arresting Capone on vagrancy charges in April 1930, a ploy that a Chicago judge repeated in September of the same year. Neither charge succeeded in achieving the desired intent.

Centre of Attention

Although he was undoubtedly a gangster who inflicted pain, suffering and death on many people, Capone didn't really see himself in the same light. He liked to portray himself as a pillar of the community and a benevolent character that helped others, opening soup kitchens during the Depression and making significant donations to numerous charities. That image was, however, the complete opposite of the view of many — particularly the law enforcement agencies.

Well-known for his brutality, Capone was described by the New Yorker in 1928 as 'the greatest gang leader in history'. Against that, he considered himself a gentleman and believed the jobs he provided, criminal though they may be, created an income for people who would otherwise be poor. He liked to be described as some sort of Robin Hood, who gave to the poor at the expense of the rich.

Many people, particularly Italian immigrants, viewed him as a community leader who helped the poor. One of his projects was to provide daily milk to poor Chicago schoolchildren to help prevent rickets. He would send flowers to the funerals of rival gang members and had a reputation for helping people who were in need.

A Sharp Dresser

Capone was a flamboyant character who wore sharp, pin stripe or chalk suits and fedora hats in lighter, contrasting colors, often with a cigar in his mouth, an image on which numerous fictitious gangster characters are based. The suits were in a variety of colors ranging from charcoal through to lighter summer colors, especially when in Florida. The suit lengths were often imported from Italy at a price that was the equivalent of $6,500 each today.

He was generally adorned with gaudy jeweler, which he dispensed with at his trial for tax evasion in order to display a more conservative image. His more human side also extended to a love of fishing, singing and writing music.

Despite his Italian roots and his membership of what was in essence a crime group with a very Italian background, Capone was fiercely American. If at any time he was described as Italian, he would proudly insist that he was born in Brooklyn.

Maintaining a High Profile

He loved his celebrity status and nourished it by always being available to talk to the press. When questioned about his activities, he portrayed himself as a respectable businessman who aimed to satisfy demand and was providing a public service by doing so.

Capone's courting of the press and his quest for publicity were things that later came back to haunt him. In interviews while in prison, he voiced regrets at having spoken so extensively to the press because the high profile that resulted had made him a target and had at the very least accelerated his eventual demise.

As well as associating with the press, Capone attended the opera, ball games and other public events where he generally was greeted with standing ovations and people wishing to shake him by the hand. Numerous attempts to increase his profile included moving the headquarters to the luxurious Metropole Hotel for a time.

For a period of four years, from 1925 to 1929, Capone was the most high profile gangster in the country. He worked hard to cultivate his image as a respectable businessman who cared for the people of Chicago. Throughout that period, however, conflicts between the rival gangs were increasing and the violence was growing, which was at variance with the image Capone strove to promote.

He ḥated the nickname of 'Scarface' that was given to him by the press, since it didn't fit with the image he wanted to put out. Instead, he preferred close friends' reference to him as 'Snorky', a slang term to describe a sharp dresser, or other criminal associates calling him the 'Big Fellow' or 'Big Al'.

Neither of the latter names referred to his height because, at five foot ten inches, he was little over average height although he was at the very least somewhat corpulent. The reference was more likely to his status as undisputed head of criminal activities in Chicago.

At the height of his fame, around 1927, his notoriety had spread throughout the country and even abroad. Tour buses drove past his headquarters, visitors expected to see him and the police even recruited him to greet a group of Italian aviators on a world tour.

Capone reputedly had a long-held belief that he would have been better selling milk than alcohol since there was a lot less hassle and an enduring demand. He did, in fact, own a dairy farm and sold milk in bottles that were labelled with expiry dates, which is something we accept as a regular occurrence today. Back then, it tied in with his stated wish for all milk sold in Chicago to have expiry dates, resulting from a relative apparently having become ill after drinking old milk and, possibly, simply being part of his wish to be seen as a respectable businessman.

Relationships with his Family

Capone was a devoted family man and tried to keep his home life entirely separate from his criminal activities, an approach advocated by his mentor Johnny Torrio. One theory is that he started or at least escalated his life of crime to provide for his family after his father died when he was only 21. He was devoted to his mother and was in daily contact with her whenever possible.

Although Capone's marriage to Mae endured right through to his death, that doesn't mean he remained faithful to her. His sexual deeds led to his contracting syphilis and he then infected his wife with the disease, never admitting he had contracted it since that would have been an admission of adultery. For the same reason, he never undertook treatment despite suffering flu-like symptoms, rashes and sores as a result of it.

The conflicting views of Al Capone once led to someone describing him as the kind of person who would kiss babies during the day and kill their parents at night while they slept. That probably just about sums up his personality and was reflected in the way he did business, negotiating with a smile on his face but destroying and killing those who refused to do business with him on his terms.

Victims and Events

Throughout Capone's career, a whole string of killings and other unsavory events were linked to his name. He was prone to mood swings and frequent violent outbursts, which with hindsight may have been brought on by the gradually worsening dementia that resulted from his syphilis infection.

According to the Chicago Daily Tribune, 33 people were killed, directly or indirectly, by Capone, while others put the figure as high as 700. The earliest of these killings, on 7th May 1923, was Joe Howard, who attempted to hijack a beer consignment belonging to Johnny Torrio and had attacked Jake 'Greasy Thumb' Guzik, the trusted treasurer and financial expert of the Outfit. There was also suspicion that Capone had been involved in the death of 'Big Jim' Colosimo three years previously.

Removing Rival Gang Leaders

At Torrio's request, Capone was believed to have participated in the killing of North Side Gang leader Dean O'Banion in November 1924. That incident resulted in Torrio being shot in a revenge attack, forcing his retirement and causing Capone's accession to the top job. It also, in October 1926, led to the murder of Earl 'Hymie' Weiss, who succeeded O'Banion as North Street Gang leader and vowed to get Capone.

Weiss was the son of Polish immigrants and had formed the North Side Gang along with

Dean O'Banion and George 'Bugs' Moran. He took over after O'Banion's death and made several attempts on Capone's life in a bid to gain revenge.

There had been a previous attempt on Weiss's life after Capone's driver was tortured and killed. Following that, on 20th September 1926, the North Side Gang made a concerted attempt to murder Capone.

After staging a ploy to draw him to the windows of his Hawthorne Inn headquarters, they then opened fire with machine guns and shotguns. Capone escaped unhurt and, after attempts to call a truce failed, Weiss and a companion were killed and three others injured three weeks later outside the North Side headquarters.

The response was to kidnap and kill the owner of the Hawthorne Inn's restaurant, who was a friend of Capone.

Although no-one was ever charged with Weiss's murder, it was widely thought that Capone's top gunman, Jack McGurn, armed with a machine gun, had been one of the two assailants. Trusted associate Frank Nitti was suspected of being responsible for the planning of the hit.

The Killing of Billy McSwiggin

On 27th April 1926, in an event that became known as the Adonis Club Massacre, Thomas Duffy and James Doherty were killed due to their threats against an attempt by Capone and Frankie Yale to bring large quantities of bootleg whiskey into Chicago.

The killings were undertaken by gunmen armed with machine guns. They drove past in five cars and opened fire as members of a rival gang left the Adonis Club bar.

Caught up in the shooting and also killed was assistant state prosecutor Billy McSwiggin, known as the 'hanging prosecutor'. McSwiggin was well-known for going after bootleggers. He had previously attempted to prosecute Capone for the murder of a rival but without success.

Although Capone was suspected but not arrested due to a lack of evidence, there was a big public outcry. That helped to turn public opinion against him and possibly, to some degree, set in motion events that would eventually lead to his downfall.

After McSwiggin's murder, Capone lay low for almost three months. Eventually, he came out of hiding and presented himself to the police. With insufficient evidence to have any hope of gaining a conviction, they had no option but to let him go, thereby increasing even further his aura of invincibility.

Killing for a Purpose

Capone viewed killing rival gang members as an act of self-defense since he was only doing it to protect his business. Although he rarely took part in the killings himself, there were incidences where he was known or suspected of having taken personal responsibility. One of these occurred on 7th May 1928, when he eliminated three men who had been part of a plot to assassinate him.

Former associates, they were invited to a banquet and plied with food and drink. Lulled into a false sense of security, they were tied to their chairs and then Capone systematically beat them to death with a baseball bat in a scene later replicated in 'The Untouchables' film.

Another dozen killings followed over the next eighteen months. Some of these were to get rid of rivals who were threatening the operation. Others were people who had been brought in to kill Capone, who had a $50,000 bounty put on his head by rival mobsters, while some planned to testify against him or did not support him as required.

Capone was rarely personally involved in the killings but ordered others to carry them out on his behalf. An exception came after an assault on friend and accomplice Jack Guzik, Capone shooting the culprit dead in a bar. An absence of witnesses meant he was never charged with the murder but his reputation grew as a result.

As Chicago became more violent, with drive-by killings increasingly frequent and innocent people caught in the cross-fire, Capone somewhat surprisingly acted as a peacemaker. He succeeded in stopping the killings and violence for around two months by arranging an amnesty between the various gangs. However, this was never likely to last long and normal activities soon resumed with street violence and fighting between the gangs.

The Treachery of Frankie Yale

A big problem was the regular hijacking of Capone's whiskey transports. This was largely blamed on Frankie Yale, Capone's long-time associate who was now seen as a rival having turned against him. This was reportedly after the appointment of Tony Lombardo as president of Unione Sicilana, an organisation that supposedly controlled much of the Italian-American vote and from which Capone's outfit received some of its political protection.

Capone had supported Lombardo's candidacy while Yale had backed Joe Aiello. Once Lombardo took over, Yale disapproved of his actions and received reduced income from the Unione. He decided to recover the shortfall from Capone and, being responsible for the safe passage of Capone's whiskey shipments through New York, he instead began to hijack some of them.

Yale was killed by machine gun fire on 1st July 1928 but not before he had ordered Capone's informant against him to be murdered. A gun used in that murder was subsequently found to be one of those acquired by Parker Henderson Junior for Capone and led to Henderson eventually testifying against Capone at his tax evasion trial

The St. Valentine's Day Massacre

The next and most notorious event of all, the St. Valentine's Day Massacre, occurred on 14th February 1929. The North Side Gang, which was now led by George Clarence 'Bugs' Moran in succession to Vincent Drucci, who had taken over on Hymie Weiss's death and then himself been killed, had long been a problem for Capone.

The violence between the North Side Gang and Torrio's South Side Gang (later to become the Chicago Outfit) really grew when the latter started selling alcohol on the North Side's territory. That ultimately led to the murder of O'Banion outside a flower shop that he owned.

The relationship between Capone and Moran gradually deteriorated, with Moran attacking Capone's premises, hijacking his liquor shipments and killing those associated with him. There were numerous attacks and retaliations, including two attempts on Capone's life by drive-by shootings, a form of attack that Moran made popular.

An attempt on the life of Capone's friend and associate, Jack McGurn, at last prompted some action. The plan was to ambush Bugs Moran at a warehouse and garage that served as the North Side Gang's headquarters. Capone's men kept watch from an apartment across the street and, on the morning of 14th February, signalled that they had seen Moran enter the premises.

Some of Capone's men, in police uniforms and a stolen police car staged a raid on the premises and lined seven men up against a wall without a struggle. They were disarmed and then shot in cold blood with machineguns and shotguns.

Six of the men were killed instantly but one, Frank Gusenberg, was still alive despite having taken fourteen bullets. He made it to the hospital but died shortly afterwards.

The main problem for Capone was that Moran, despite the information given to him, was not among the victims. Having seen the police car pull up outside the warehouse, he had made his getaway before the attack took place. All Capone's further attempts to get Moran failed, the gangster eventually dying of lung cancer while serving the second of two ten-year jail sentences for bank robbery.

Aftermath of the St. Valentine's Day Massacre

The atrocity caused public outrage and prompted intense police activity. Up to that point, people had tolerated Prohibition and the lawlessness that came with it. Most of the associated violence revolved around gangsters shooting other gangsters, with usually no direct effect on the general public.

Although this event was really no different, the scale and brutality of the killing caused uproar. Photographs of the aftermath of the attack showed the outcome with gruesome reality, causing a demand for something to be done. That drove President Herbert

Hoover to resolve to make an example of Capone.

Although Capone was suspected of being behind the killings, he was at his mansion in Florida when they took place and supposedly had a note from his doctor confirming that he was confined to his bed. Nevertheless, it is widely believed that Capone planned the Saint Valentine's Day Massacre from his Florida mansion. McGurn was checked into a distant hotel and there was no evidence of either man's involvement, resulting in no-one ever being convicted of the crimes.

McGurn was staying at the hotel with his then girlfriend, Louise Rolfe, who claimed they had spent the whole day together in bed. Nevertheless, the police charged him with the seven murders and subsequently also charged him with crossing state lines with Rolfe, an offence at the time due to her being an unmarried woman. McGurn prevented her testifying against him by divorcing his wife and marrying Rolfe, resulting in all charges being dropped.

McGurn was later named Public Enemy Number Four at the time Capone was Number One on the list. However, he subsequently became ostracized by Capone's outfit and in 1936 was shot and killed.

The main suspects for that killing were Bugs Moran, as revenge for McGurn's part in the St. Valentine's Day Massacre, or the Chicago Outfit because he knew too much about them. McGurn was buried at Mount Carmel Cemetery in Hillside, Illinois, the same resting place as many other gangsters, including Al Capone.

The public reaction to the St. Valentine's Day Massacre added to the determination to convict Capone and was another contributory factor in his eventual downfall. He was summoned to appear before a grand jury in connection with the massacre but failed to attend, claiming he was unwell.

He was finally, in 1931, charged with contempt of court for that failure to appear and ultimately did receive a one-year jail sentence that he served after completing his time for the tax evasion charges. More crucially, since a federal court issued the contempt citation, the FBI became involved and it was their work that eventually brought about his downfall.

An estimated seven further killings took place over the next eighteen months up to 23rd October 1930 before he was found guilty of tax fraud the following year.

The Quest for Justice

Al Capone ruled by terror and murder for many years and was pursued by the police for numerous crimes without success. It is, therefore, somewhat ironic that he was eventually convicted and jailed for something as comparatively simple and harmless as tax evasion.

How Capone Evaded Justice

He avoided prosecution for a long time by a process of bribery and corruption of police and officials combined with intimidating or eliminating potential witnesses. An estimated $30 million was spent in 1927 on bribes to various people who could protect him in some way.

His own employees or associates were either fiercely loyal to him or were too fearful for their own safety to act against him. Although many people knew of his crimes, hardly any of them were prepared to say anything about them. He was also careful not to be linked with criminal acts, ensured alibis were watertight and had no properties registered in his name.

Capone dealt exclusively in cash, having no bank account in his name and apparently only ever signing one cheque (for a gambling debt), so that no transactions could be traced back to him. Nevertheless, the case against him was building slowly (the one cheque in his name being part of the evidence) and the outcome seemed increasingly inevitable.

Gaining the First Convictions

Public outcry against his activities became so great that, in March 1929, President Herbert Hoover insisted to Secretary of the Treasury Andrew Mellon that Capone must be jailed. That started the process that would eventually lead to him being convicted of tax evasion.

Prior to that, Capone's first conviction for a criminal offence came in May 1929 after he was arrested in Philadelphia for carrying a concealed weapon while on his way back from a meeting of crime bosses in Atlantic City, New Jersey. He was convicted and sentenced, within sixteen hours of his arrest, to one year in jail but was freed in March 1930 for good behavior.

One month later, Capone was named Public Enemy Number 1 by the Chicago Crime Commission when it released its first list of wanted criminals. This didn't help the reputation of a man who wanted to be viewed as a solid citizen and businessman.

The Role of Eliot Ness

Federal agent Eliot Ness has been widely credited with bringing about Capone's downfall. That's largely due to his memoirs, 'The Untouchables', which subsequently gave rise to a successful TV series and film, although it is now accepted that his role was somewhat exaggerated. The responsibility for this is largely accredited to co-author Oscar Fraley, who was the source of many of the 'facts' in the book.

Ness's small team of prohibition agents was labelled 'the Untouchables' because they supposedly could not be bribed. They raided illegal breweries and other illicit operations and were involved in Capone's indictment for prohibition violations when he was arrested after testifying to a grand jury on 27th March 1929.

Indeed, Ness's team was able to assemble a bootlegging indictment against Capone that ran to 5,000 charges. That work went to waste to some degree when the decision was later taken to prosecute on tax evasion charges instead.

Ness did succeed in angering Capone greatly by destroying or seizing millions of dollars' worth of brewing equipment, destroying thousands of gallons of alcohol, closing some large breweries and damaging his bootlegging business by exposing prohibition violations. A lot of the increased activity was undertaken after Capone murdered a friend of Ness.

Ness's Innovative Methods

Ness was at the very least innovative in his methods and beliefs. His squad cars were painted in easily recognizable colors and had two-way radios to make communication easy. He pioneered forensic science, with an emphasis on ballistic tests and soil samples, and made use of wiretapping to gather evidence.

His battle against corruption led to the setting up of teams to investigate the bribery of police officers, the forerunner of today's internal affairs divisions. And his views on alcohol and drug addiction were ahead of his time, believing that they were medical problems rather than being treated as criminal acts, as was then the prevalent thought.

Although Ness was certainly above bribery and corruption, he wasn't quite the saintly figure that was portrayed. Some of the alcohol that was impounded was given away to reporters to encourage them to cover the story and Ness himself was partial to a drink. His later years featured periods of heavy drinking after a spell as Cleveland's director of public safety and a failed attempt in 1947 to become Cleveland's mayor, before his death in 1957 at the age of 55.

Ness's death occurred shortly before 'The Untouchables' book was published Although a lot of the content was fictitious nonsense, the book told a great story and was a huge success. As were, of course, the TV series starring Robert Stack as Ness, which ran for four years from 1959, and the film starring Kevin Costner that grossed $76 million.

The Change of Tactics

One of the reasons that Capone evaded justice for so long was that different agencies were responsible for investigating his various activities and the FBI only became involved latterly. Any prohibition offences, for example, were the responsibility of the Bureau of Prohibition while the killings in the St. Valentine's Day Massacre were not classed as federal offences.

In an attempt to run Capone out of Florida, he was arrested on vagrancy charges in April 1930. In February 1931, he was tried for contempt as a result of him failing to attend a grand jury hearing after feigning illness. He was sentenced to six months in jail but was freed while he appealed the conviction.

This was the first time the FBI became involved in the pursuit of Al Capone, being asked by US Attorneys to find out if his excuse of ill-health was genuine. It proved not to be true since, despite Capone being supposedly bed-ridden at the time while suffering from bronchopneumonia, he was spotted at the race track, on holiday and was even being questioned by local prosecutors during that period. That resulted in him being cited for contempt of court and other charges followed on from there.

Preparing for the Tax Evasion Charge

A lot of the credit for Capone's later conviction for tax evasion goes to Elmer Irey, a United States Treasury Department official who was told by Secretary of the Treasury Andrew Mellon that it was the responsibility of his office to put Capone in jail. He led the Internal Revenue Service's investigative unit that built a case against him. That was only possible due to a change of law in 1927 when the Supreme Court decreed that income tax was due on illegal earnings.

This occurred during a trial against bootlegger Manley Sullivan, who was convicted of failing to file a tax return that showed the profits he made from his criminal businesses. An argument that the Fifth Amendment protected criminals from having to report illegal earnings was rejected by Justice Oliver Wendell Holmes Junior.

This cleared the way for the IRS special investigation unit to appoint Frank J Wilson, their most relentless and aggressive investigator, to investigate Capone. He was to focus on his spending as a means of proving his level of income.

Capone's income was obviously substantial since his net worth was estimated at about $30 million in 1929. Despite this, he had never filed an income tax return.

Capone had long maintained to all who would listen that he was a respectable and successful businessman. The main point he had overlooked, however, was that successful businessmen earn a good income and have to pay their taxes on that income. That was a big hole in Capone's record that the government looked to exploit.

Lavish Spending Was the Key

Capone's income was well hidden due to the lack of a bank account and no record of any assets in his name. Consequently, Wilson's team of five investigators concentrated initially on his extravagant lifestyle and uncovered purchases of Lincoln limousines, gold plated dinner services and jewel studded belt buckles. They also found evidence of the booking of luxury hotel suites, the staging of lavish parties and telephone bills amounting to $39,000.

Such levels of spending could only be possible if there was the income to match it but determining that income was little short of impossible. Although the revenue came from hundreds of sources, there was no obvious documentary evidence and no-one willing to testify against Capone. That was due to a sense of loyalty or, more likely in many cases, a fear of their lives or well-being should they dare to talk.

One who did talk was Eddie O'Hare, an operator of dog racing tracks and patent owner of the mechanical lure used in these events. He provided leads for the investigators but eventually paid with his life when he was shot to death just before Capone was released from prison.

Breakthroughs in the Investigation

The investigation ran for two years and the first real breakthrough, in 1930, was the acquisition of three bound ledgers found in a raid on one of Capone's premises. These ledgers appeared to provide evidence of income from a gambling hall although without conclusive proof that they referred to Capone.

Comparison of handwriting in the ledgers identified the author as Leslie Shumway and, having tracked him down to his Florida home; agents threatened him with a subpoena. Aware of the trouble he was in, with Capone certain to exact retribution if he were to divulge information, Shumway took protection and agreed to talk. He submitted an affidavit where he described the gambling business and admitted he took orders from Capone in relation to it.

Another important witness was Frank Reis, who was named on several cashier cheques that were assumed to be intended for Capone. After spending four days in solitary confinement, he admitted to agents that he was employed by Capone and that the cheques covered profits at his Cicero gambling hall. This evidence was later repeated in testimony to a grand jury.

In the trial that followed in 1931, the ledgers were actually inadmissible due to the statute of limitations. However, Capone's lawyers failed to make the necessary objections, although the ledgers themselves did not prove his control of the business.

Around this time, Capone's Brother Ralph was tried and convicted of tax evasion. He was sentenced to three years in prison and this prompted Al Capone to take action so the same didn't happen to him.

Capone's Crucial Mistake that Led to his Conviction

He instructed his lawyers to regularize his tax situation but, in doing so, gave the authorities the information they needed about his income. Capone was present at a meeting, in April 1930, between his tax attorney Lawrence Mattingly and investigator Frank Wilson when the stated intention was to settle his tax dues.

At that meeting, Capone nevertheless refused to admit the level of his income and grew increasingly irritated as it progressed, eventually issuing a thinly veiled threat against Wilson and his wife. Five months later, on 30th September, Capone's lawyers stated in a letter that he was willing to pay tax on income in a specific number of years.

This letter covered the six years that were in dispute. It offered that he would pay tax on Capone's income in that period, ranging from an admitted $26,000 in 1924 through to $100,000 in each of the years 1928 and 1929.

The government now had the documentary evidence it so badly needed of Capone's large amounts of income over several years. It was a grave mistake on Capone's part and resulted in him being charged in 1931 with tax evasion as well as violations of the Volstead Act (Prohibition).

The charges were backed up by other evidence gathered by Elmer Irey's team, agents having infiltrated Capone's organization at great risk to themselves. One informer was killed before he could testify but the two bookkeepers who had been employed by Capone were put under police protection before charges were brought.

The Charges against Capone

The government initially claimed Capone had a 1924 tax liability of more than $32,000, while still investigating the years 1925 to 1929. The grand jury indicted Capone for the 1924 evasion of income tax two days before the statute of limitations would have prevented this. Further counts covering the years 1925 to 1929 were added two months later.

Ultimately, the grand jury found Capone guilty of 22 counts of tax evasion in the sum of over $200,000. Additionally, he and 68 gang members were charged with 5,000 violations of the Volstead Act but the tax evasion charges were considered to have precedence over these.

These were reckoned to have the far greatest chance of success since many jurors would be likely to drink alcohol and therefore have some sympathy with Capone's activities. However, such approval was unlikely to extend to tax evasion, which was generally a detested offence.

The Plea Bargain that Failed

With doubts over the six-year statute of limitations being upheld by the Supreme Court and fears that witnesses could intimidated, US Attorney George E Q Johnson arranged a plea bargain that could see Capone being jailed for as little as two years and no more than five years.

Judge James Herbert Wilkerson, however, would have none of this and refused to allow the deal, so Capone withdrew his guilty plea. Wilkerson was keen to stress that there would be no bargaining with the Federal Government and that the parties involved in a criminal case could not determine the judgment.

How Jury Intimidation was Avoided

Instead, the trial went ahead and a vital element was Judge Wilkerson changing the jury for a fresh one at the last minute and sequestering them each night to prevent them being bribed or intimidated. The action came after the Judge learned that Capone's organization had managed to obtain a full list of all the prospective jurors and was engaged in giving out bribes and making threats to get them on his side.

That knowledge was provided by informant Eddie O'Hare to Frank Wilson, who was initially doubtful of the claims. O'Hare was able to provide a list of ten names, however, that matched those on the list of jurors that even Judge Wilkerson hadn't yet been given.

Wilson was worried that all the work done to bring Capone to trial would be wasted but his fears were allayed by Wilkerson, who was apparently unconcerned by the development. On 5th October 1931, the first day of the trial, Judge Wilkerson started proceedings by exchanging his panel of jurors for another at a trial that was due to start that day in another court.

Capone, who had smiled at the jurors as he walked into court with his bodyguards, was visibly taken aback by this turn of events. The 23 charges of tax evasion against him were then outlined in front of the twelve jurors — all men, since female jurors were not allowed in Illinois until 1939.

The Evidence Against Capone

As various witnesses were called, the evidence against Capone slowly mounted. Tax collector Charles W Arndt affirmed that Capone had not filed any tax returns for the years 1924 to 1929 while Cicero citizen Chester Bragg testified that Capone had clearly stated that he was the owner of the Hawthorne Smoke Shop, a Cicero gambling hall.

That occurred during a citizens' raid on the place and the Reverend Henry Hoover, who led the raid, recalled that Capone had threatened the participants. Some of the most damning evidence came from Leslie Shumway, who had been the cashier at the Hawthorne Smoke Shop. He estimated that profits of over $550,000 accrued during the two years he worked there but was reluctant to identify Capone as the owner, although he did confirm he was in charge of the business.

Crucial to the case was Judge Wilkerson allowing the letter from Capone's lawyers to be admitted into evidence. He over-ruled an objection that, in effect, a lawyer could not make a confession on behalf of his client. This followed agent Frank Wilson's description of Lawrence Mattingly delivering the letter and stating that Capone was willing to pay the tax liability arising from the income shown on it.

Lengthy evidence of Capone's spending was presented by US Attorney Johnson and he emphasized the hypocrisy of someone who, while claiming to be a man of the people, spent obscene amounts of money on himself and gave relatively little to others. More crucially, the high levels of spending were evidence of the income that Capone achieved but did not declare to the tax authorities.

Evidence of Capone's lavish spending came from several witnesses. One of these was Parker Henderson Junior, who had acted as Capone's real estate representative. He recalled that he'd shown Capone several properties in Florida, resulting in him buying the mansion on Palm Island. Another witness testified to seeing large amounts of cash at the property.

Similarly, a clerk at the Metropole Hotel in Chicago told how Capone held lavish parties there and booked the most expensive suites. All of this was paid for in cash, in large denomination bills.

Frank Reis, cashier at the Hawthorne Smoke Shop in 1927, reckoned the profits there that year were about $150,000. This money was used to purchase a large number of cashier's cheques, at least one of which bore Al Capone's signature.

Failure of the Defence Case

Once the prosecution had presented its evidence, the defense took only one day to make its case and did not do a very good job. Having failed to object to the ledgers being brought into evidence due to the statute of limitations, it then presented a mistaken defense based on gambling losses.

It depicted Capone as a gambling addict who had lost the money his business had earned. Since gambling losses could only be offset against winnings, however, this didn't excuse him from paying tax on his business income.

The defense case that Capone had lost $327,000 over six years and this matched his taxable income was totally spurious. In summing up, defense attorney Albert Fink denied there was sufficient evidence of Capone's gross income and accused the government of being determined to convict him at all costs. Whilst pleading that the jury should not convict Capone just because he was a bad person, he also tried to depict his good side and said he was not a tax cheat.

In his summing up, prosecutor Jacob Grossman stressed that Capone's lavish spending was obvious evidence of a very large income and that the letter submitted by lawyer Mattingly proved that Capone knew he had committed tax evasion. US Attorney George Jackson claimed the case would establish whether someone could conduct his affairs in such a way that he was above the law.

The Verdict that Ended Capone's Criminal Career

On 17th October 1931, after deliberating for only nine hours, the jury found Al Capone guilty of tax evasion on several counts. Although he was acquitted on most counts and found guilty of only five, these were enough for the judge to hand down a sentence that was far above the normal level for this type of offence.

He was sentenced to eleven years in jail and ordered to pay court costs of $30,000 and $50,000 in fines as well as the $215,000 plus interest he owed in back taxes. This was the harshest sentence ever imposed for tax fraud, one that visibly shocked Capone and his lawyers.

To appeal the conviction, Capone appointed a Washington-based law firm that was expert in tax law. They filed a writ of habeas corpus, stating that the charges were outside the time limit for prosecution due to the Supreme Court having ruled that tax evasion was not classed as fraud. The judge over-ruled the appeal by deducting the time Capone had spent in Miami from the length of time since the offences.

Effect of the Conviction

That was the end of Capone's criminal career. His role within organized crime in Chicago ceased immediately although the organization he had previously headed simply carried on under new leadership. A succession of bosses followed him, chiefly Frank Nitti, Paul Ricca, Tony Accardo and

Sam Giancana from amongst his previous followers.

The level of violence decreased, however, and Capone's successors adopted a lower profile than he had done. With the end of Prohibition in 1933, the extent of the criminal activities naturally diminished. Nevertheless, the levels of gambling, prostitution and various other illegal activities continued pretty much as before.

One perhaps surprising consequence of Capone's conviction was that back tax receipts went up, both from criminals and law-abiding citizens. That year, the value of unpaid tax filings paid doubled to over $1 million compared to the previous year.

Final Days

In May 1932, at the age of 33 and weighing almost 18 stones, Capone arrived at Atlanta US Penitentiary. A medical examination there revealed that the use of cocaine had perforated his septum and he was suffering from withdrawal symptoms as a result of his addiction. He was also diagnosed as having syphilis and gonorrhoea, the results of his time working in brothels, and which would lead to further deterioration in his health.

His mental health was already showing signs of failing and he was seen as a weak personality who could not deal with bullying. He required the protection of cellmate Red Rudinsky, formerly a minor associate of Capone's gang, which drew accusations of special treatment.

This belief of favoritism was borne out by the conditions under which he lived. Despite his delicate mental state, he was able to use his influence to procure special privileges, furnishings and other items that made his life easier.

His cell had a carpet, personal bedding and other expensive furnishings. There was also a radio and Capone and various inmates and guards would converse and listen to favorite programs. Visitors were plentiful, with friends and family members maintaining a residence in a nearby hotel.

The Transfer to Alcatraz

Partly because of this, and also to provide publicity for the newly opened Alcatraz Federal Penitentiary in San Francisco Bay, Capone was moved there in June 1936. Alcatraz was a maximum security prison intended for violent inmates or those with disciplinary issues. Capone did not fall into those categories so the gaining of publicity for the new facility seemed the most logical reason for moving him there.

Soon after arriving at Alcatraz, Capone was stabbed and slightly wounded by another inmate. The assailant was James 'Tex' Lucas, a 22-year old Texan who was serving thirty years in federal prison for auto theft and bank robbery.

He turned out to be a trouble-maker after transferring to Alcatraz from Leavenworth, since he was later involved in a work strike followed by a violent escape attempt in which a prison officer was killed. Lucas received a life sentence for that and a spell in solitary confinement.

The attack on Capone, on 23rd June 1936, was, he alleged, in response to a threat to kill Lucas. He attacked Capone in the shower room, striking him with one half of a pair of scissors and inflicting superficial cuts to his chest and hands. For the offence, Lucas lost his accumulated time for good behavior, a total of 3,600 days.

During his time in Alcatraz, Capone remained a celebrity. There were constant questions from the press regarding his well-being, activities and anything else about him. Even many years after his death, the cell he occupied is one of the main visitor attractions on 'the Rock'.

Capone's syphilis caused the onset of dementia and eroded his mental capacity. The doctors tried to eradicate the syphilis with malaria injections, hoping the induced fever would clear it.

The treatment almost killed Capone and he spent the last twelve months at Alcatraz in the prison hospital in a confused state. On 6th January 1939, he was released and transferred to the Federal Correctional Institution at Terminal Island near Los

Angeles, to serve a twelve-month sentence for the contempt of court conviction.

Release from Prison and Hospital Treatment

Capone was paroled on 16th November 1939 and referred to John Hopkins Hospital in Baltimore for treatment of syphilis-related illnesses. Admission was refused because of who he was and instead he was admitted to the Union Memorial Hospital. There he became one of the first civilian patients to be administered penicillin as treatment for his syphilis, although by now the condition was far too advanced for it to have much effect.

After several weeks of in-patient and out-patient treatment, Capone left Baltimore on 20th March 1940, donating two Japanese weeping cherry trees to the hospital as thanks for the care he had received. He returned to his mansion on Palm Island for the remaining years of his life, passing the time playing cards and fishing. Test conducted in 1946 by his physician and a psychiatrist concluded that he had the mental capacity of a twelve-year old child.

Capone spent his final days being cared for by his wife and brothers. Most of his time was spent wearing pajamas and having conversations with enemies and colleagues who had died years before, some of them on his orders.

He was reportedly paid by the Outfit a salary of $600 a week, which was barely enough to support his family, pay his staff and maintain the property. Wife Mae kept him in isolation during his last years, knowing any loose public statements about his old organization could well cost him his life while violent outburst brought on by his condition would lose him his freedom.

Illness and Death

Capone suffered a stroke on 21st January 1947. Although he began to recover, he then contracted pneumonia and, on 22nd January, suffered a cardiac arrest.

He died three days later at the age of 48 with his family around him and his physician asked if an autopsy could be conducted on his brain and body for the purposes of medical research. This was refused by the family and the body went to the Philbrick

Funeral Home in Miami Beach where it was placed in a $2,000 massive bronze casket.

The body was available for viewing by permitted guests only although two funeral home employees apparently took surreptitious photographs of Al Capone lying in his open coffin. Huge quantities of flowers arrived and the funeral service was held the following Wednesday at St. Patrick's Roman Catholic Church.

Final Resting Place

Capone was buried at Mount Olivet Cemetery in Chicago close to his father and one brother. Three years afterwards, to counter the constant attention and the vandalism of the gravestone, all the family remains were removed to Mount Carmel

Cemetery in Hillside, Illinois. The original monument was left in place in Mount Olivet Cemetery in an unsuccessful attempt to prevent visitors learning of the new location of the remains.

In a strange twist of fate, Capone died only five days after Andrew John Volstead at the age of 86. Volstead was a member of the United States House of Representatives who, while serving as chairman of the House Judiciary Committee, co-authored the National Prohibition Act of 1916 that bears his name. The act enabled the enforcement of Prohibition, with Capone's subsequent criminal career partly based on the evasion of that legislation.

Mae continued to live in the Palm Island mansion for another five years until she was forced to sell it. She died in 1986, aged 89, but not before she had destroyed all her diaries and private papers relating to Al Capone.

The Capone Legacy

Despite Capone's violent career and the brutality of his past, there is an on-going fascination with his life. Many fictitious characters have been modelled on him and the term 'mobster' or 'gangster' invariably conjures up an image of Al Capone.

There have been plenty of books and articles covering his life and some of these have been made into films. The most well-known of these is Eliot Ness's biography 'The Untouchables', which subsequently became a successful TV series and then a major film. As in many cases, however, the facts weren't always faithfully recorded and the roles of individuals are sometimes exaggerated.

In real life, Capone's influence was enough to change the law in order to deal with him. The 1927 Supreme Court ruling that income tax was due on criminal earnings was intended to help the authorities trap criminals and was instrumental in Capone's eventual downfall.

The End of Prohibition

Later on, the end of the Prohibition era in 1933 was brought about because many Americans enjoyed going to a speakeasy and having a drink. Additionally, it was obvious that Prohibition was actually encouraging criminal activity and many gangsters were getting rich through their bootlegging activities.

So maybe Al Capone's greatest legacy is, ironically, that through violence and brutality, he changed the laws of America. In order to stop him and his peers, activities that he'd undertaken illegally were made legal.

Although there are the contrasting images that Capone leaves behind — on the one hand a do-gooder who helped the poor and on the other a mobster who thought nothing of torturing and killing his opponents — many of his relatives have responded to the bad side. Some have changed their names and moved away from Chicago while others have refused to talk about him or have done so only under the cover of anonymity.

Despite his notoriety as a mobster, one of the biggest ironies of all is that Capone spent longer in jail than he did as a leading criminal. His reign as a crime boss ended after six years at the age of 33. He was then to spend the next seven years six months and fifteen days in prison before his eventual release on parole.

Ongoing Fascination with Capone

The fascination with Capone appears to show little sign of slackening, even seventy years after his death. A recent auction in June 2017 saw a diamond studded platinum pocket watch that belonged to him sold for $84,375.

The triangular watch, on a fourteen carat white gold chain, features 23 diamonds in the shape of his initials, surrounded by a further 26 diamonds and another 72 diamonds on the watch face. Also sold at the auction, for $18,750, was a musical composition — 'Humanesque' — written by Capone in pencil while imprisoned in Alcatraz.

In September 2016, a letter from Capone sold for $62,500 at an auction in Massachusetts. Written to his son from his cell in Alcatraz, the letter, according to experts, showed Capone's softer side.

The Chicago History Museum's website still gets 50,000 hits a month on pages about Capone while visitors to Chicago still drive past his old home and visit his grave site, even though the body is no longer there.

However, the city has made little effort to publicize or preserve the sites associated with Capone, not wishing to draw attention to its violent past.

Capone's Palm Island estate sold for $7.4 million in 2014. It is now available for hire to use for private functions or events, so the fascination with Capone still endures.

THE KRAYS

Britain's Most Notorious Gangsters

Roger Harrington

Part 1 – Childhood

London, East End, 1945.

The East End of London in the 1940s was a post-war landscape. Poverty and crime were rife. People struggled to make ends meet and opportunities to escape were few and far between.

Houses were cramped due to increased immigration and from the bombing during the war. Food was still scarce as rationing didn't end until 1954 and cheese production was slow for many years after. In addition to this the Suez crisis leads to a period of petrol rationing from late 1956 until May 1957.

All of this leads to a feeling of unease about people's futures. No-one knew where the next full meal was coming from. The black market was in full force, although this was not a new phenomenon.

The East End of London was a notorious breeding ground for criminals from as far back as the 17th century, so it wasn't limited to just the aftermath of the war causing social issues. The high levels of poverty in the area made it an easy way to make a living when jobs were scarce.

Some people resorted to collecting scrap to increase their income, while others resorted to less legal ways to achieve financial stability. Extortion rackets, muggings and random acts of violence made the streets of the East End a largely unsafe place. The streets became notorious for dangerous activity and the shadow of violence was always around the next corner.

Of course the notoriety didn't become a national sensation until the 1950s and 1960s, when arguably the most famous East End gangsters were plying their trade; Ronald and Reginald Kray - The Kray Twins.

Ronald and Reginald Kray, or Ronnie and Reggie as they came to be known, were born on the 24th of October 1933 to Charles Kray and Violet Lee. Reggie was the older of the two identical twins by ten minutes.

Born in Hoxton the twins moved to Bethnal Green in 1938. When the Second World War broke out, the twins' father was called up to the army and decided it would be better to go into hiding than join the front line.

The twins had an elder brother Charles junior, who was six when they were born, as well as a sister, Violet, who had died while still a baby.

Charles senior was rarely around while the twins grew up, as he worked as a travelling trader, buying and selling valuable metal and clothes as well as being in hiding due to being called up to the army, this lead to the twins being brought up by their mother, Violet.

Violet was a warm and compassionate woman, who in the absence of the twins' father dedicated her life to her children. Ensuring that they were always well dressed and trying to instill good values, respect and to make sure that they treated others less fortunate than themselves with compassion.

Other members of the family that lived in close proximity to the twins were their maternal grandparents, who lived over the road from the Krays, and their maternal aunts - Mary and Rose, who lived in the houses either side of them.

Rose was the twins' favorite aunt, possibly because she indulged them, or possibly because her own violent temper mirrored what theirs' would eventually become. When Ronnie was teased at school about having eyebrows that were very close together, she thought it was an omen and told him he was "born to be hanged".

At the age of three, both Ronnie and Reggie suffered with a serious case of diphtheria. This was especially worrying as their younger sister had died as from a similar ailment as an infant. Fortunately, for Violet they both pulled through, although Reggie made a swifter recovery than his twin.

Their father would regularly visit the house while on the run, but with the police and army regularly calling upon the house his visits became less and less frequent. The twins attributed their father not visiting to the regular appearance of the men in uniform. This would later cause them to have a deep-seated disdain for such authoritative figures which they carried with them into their adult lives.

Their father had associated with many local East End criminals and this association - as well as their ingrained hatred for authority - had a significant influence on their later life choices. Especially with the feeling of being able to do no wrong that they got from the unconditional love their mother always showered them with.

The first school the twins attended was Wood Close School. The outbreak of the Second World War would break up their education and they were then evacuated to Suffolk. This, as well as their father going into hiding, made their childhood one of constant upheaval and uncertainty.

The Kray twins enjoyed living in Suffolk, but Violet missed her family. Eventually, she decided that they would all move back home. The twins were crushed, they went back to school and began to take become interested in boxing; a family tradition.

Their maternal grandfather, Jimmy Lee, was a former bare knuckle fighter. Their father, although he had dodged conscription, came from a long line of boxers and wasn't one to back down from a fight. Their brother Charlie taught them how to box, and their natural aptitude for physical violence became apparent.

Their father took them to the Robert Browning youth club for boxing lessons as often as he could and the twins progressed at a rapid pace to become very competent fighters.

In 1948 Reggie became the schoolboy boxing champion of London and reached the finals of the Great Britain schoolboy championships. Ronnie was similarly gifted although he didn't quite achieve the same accolades as his brother.

Charlie said the twins were very different fighters, with Reggie being more calculated and skillful and Ronnie always being all guns blazing and fighting until he couldn't fight anymore.

There are varying reports on how successful the twins were as amateurs. Some accounts say they never lost a bout, although the fact that Reggie did not win the Great Britain Schoolboy finals disproves this claim. In addition to this, they are said to regularly have fought each other, but there is no record of a result of such incidents. What is certain, however, is that the twins were very skilled fighters.

The twins eventually turned professional. They would later claim that a fight at travelling fairground whey they were pitted against each other was their first professional bout, but as it was an unlicensed exhibition, the match didn't enter the record books.

Both twins were successful in the bouts they did compete in. Ronnie fought in six fights and managed to win four, Reggie, the more skilled of the two and with more amateur accolades, fought in six and won six.

The twins' brother, Charlie, was also an accomplished boxer. He kept a punching bag in his grandfather's house and regularly trained at the local boxing gym. In 1951, all three Kray brothers fought on the same bill, and Charlie was the only one to lose his fight. This would turn out to be his last fight, and it wouldn't be long until the twins ceased boxing altogether, although for very different reasons.

The twins didn't just keep their fighting in the ring. There was a lot of gang activity in the East End of London and the twins were willing participants in any kind of violence. They kept weapons on hand at all times as well as a cache of implements stashed in their bedroom.

At the age of sixteen, the twins were charged with GBH for a violent confrontation between two gangs. Although charged, the twins were acquitted due to lack of evidence. Some say that a character reference from a local vicar, who the twins ran errands for, helped them out immensely. Others feel that the witnesses had been "got to" and were persuaded to not testify in court.

At seventeen, the twins again found themselves in front of the courts. After Ronnie had an altercation with a policeman who had pushed him, both twins got involved in resisting arrest and were therefore charged with assault; another helpful hand from the local vicar lead to them only receiving probation.

The trouble with the law had not stopped their boxing career, although a solid conviction may have. In fact, the story of the Kray twins could have been very different - with them being successful boxers - were it not for the next significant event in their lives.

It was the second of March 1952 that the twins were called up for national service. A two year military duty that was mandatory for all 18 year olds in England at the time. The twins thought that they could put up with the two years if the army allowed them to take on an easy role; something akin to fitness instruction was their intended role.

Unfortunately, this never came to fruition as yet another case of bad choices; bad luck and the dislike for uniformed authority figures reared its ugly head. They had an altercation with a training officer which lead to them running back home after they had physically attacked him. The police then arrested them the following day, and this event star a long two years either in hiding, or inside military prisons.

While on the run, the twins ran into yet more trouble with the law when they assaulted a police officer. This time they ended up in jail, albeit with no vicar to rescue them. A month in Wormwood Scrubs followed by them being sent back to the army to be court martialed. The Krays would then, yet again, stage a daring escape from military grounds.

However, this time they were recaptured less than a day later and the rest of their national service was spent locked up at Shepton Mallet.

It was here, locked up at Shepton Mallet, that the twins met a different breed of men. Men more in tune with their attitude of disdain toward authority, and especially authority in uniform. One of these men in particular was Charlie Richardson, who the twins would come to have many dealings with in the future, culminating in becoming rivals in the gang scene in London.

After they were finally released from Shepton Mallet, the twins spent a year taking on small-time crime jobs. Odd jobs such as working in protection rackets and working as bouncers at the nightclubs owned by local criminals became their most common source of income. It was during these jobs where the Krays came up with their idea for the next stage in their advancement. They had ambitions of becoming bosses of the criminal underworld.

The twins elder brother, Charlie, loaned them some money to take on the lease of a run-down snooker club. It was a rough place, often the scene of multiple fights and regularly had broken glass covering the floor on the morning after a particularly raucous evening. The club was named The Regal which, before the twins took over, could be considered quite an ironic name for such an establishment. However, once the Krays took on ownership of The Regal, it suddenly became a club without trouble. Whether this was because of the fearsome reputation that the twins had cultivated, or because the twins were the ones who smashed it up so often is a question that will never be answered.

It was during this time that the twins began to take on the image of 'gangsters'. Smart suits, large rings and heavy watches all became part of their image. Even though the trouble had long since stopped at their club, the twins did nothing to dissuade the more undesirable elements of society from frequenting their establishment.

People who had been released from jail, old army friends, tough men and boys from the estate - the twins welcomed them all into The

Regal with open arms. This allowed the twins to repel any type of protection racket being launched on their club. The one occasion such an incident did occur was when a Maltese gang attempted to extort the twins. The luckiest of the men simply had his hand speared with a bayonet, while the rest of the gang all left the club much closer to death than when they entered.

It was during their ownership of The Regal that the twins started to branch out into other areas of criminal activity. They hijacked lorries which had numerous desirable products loaded on them. With the black market still thriving in an only-recently post-ration Britain, there was both a ready supply and many customers for the twins' illicit goods.

The twins began to use The Regal as more than just a legitimate business. It became a front for their criminal activities. Local villains used the club as a meeting place to formulate plans, the back room became a storage area for stolen goods and the twins became a go-between for people to fence their stolen goods. Even if they themselves were not involved in the stealing of the goods, they still took a cut of any deal that took place on their premises.

The two young upstarts in the criminal world were beginning to make a name for themselves. More established gangsters were starting to notice their antics, most of the local crime bosses ignored them, but some were less than impressed.

The twins had attracted the attention of three brothers who worked on the docks. They were the established bosses of the area and they were not happy with Ronnie and Reggie cutting into their business. As is commonplace within the crime world, a cryptic message was sent to the twins. They were invited for a Sunday morning drink at the pub that the brothers regularly drank in.

Ronnie and Reggie knew that this would be the first test of their mettle in the criminal world, both mentally and physically. The twins arrived at the pub and entered the private bar. The three dockers were drinking, and all three were physically more intimidating than Ronnie and Reggie were. The twins closed the door behind them and proceeded to obliterate the three men in front of them. When the pub manager opened the door to see the aftermath, he was shocked to see two of the dockers out cold and one being brutally pummelled by Ronnie.

By 1956 the twins had begun to run an expanding criminal empire. At this point, the twins were still only 22 years of age and yet were running a section of the capital city of England. Ronnie helped to protect their fearsome reputation and Reggie was the brains behind their rapid expansion. They soon began to skim from the top of other criminals' earnings, taking a percentage of anything that was earned on the area that they ran.

During the twins rise up the ladder of crime, the East End of London had been run by two men: Billy Hill and Jack Spot. The pair had an uneasy alliance with one another and it was only a matter of time before their relationship would come to a head. When they eventually did fall out, Jack Spot was attacked and, in the aftermath of the attack, called on the twins for support. Ronnie and Reggie were only too happy to support Jack Spot, seeing this as an opportunity to both speed up their rise and learn from someone who was experienced in the ways of gangland crime.

The twins saw this as a real opportunity for them to graduate into the big leagues, but this all changed in May 1956 when Jack Spot was attacked again. This time it was outside his apartment, and was also in the presence of his wife. Jack's face was slashed and, due to his substantial injuries, decided to make a complete career change. Jack Spot then bought a legitimate furniture store and turned his life around with no criminal activity to speak of.

In a strange twist of fate, Billy Hill also decided to retire, which left an opening at the top of the crime totem pole. This left space which was soon filled with new gangs, either remnants of Spot and Hill's old gangs, or new ones who had decided to take advantage of a potentially explosive situation. The main worry for the twins was a gang of Italians who were rumored to be targeting Ronnie and Reggie.

Deciding that attack is the best form of defense, the twins made plans to ambush the Italians at the social club they used as a base. Driving there with various members of their gang, Ronnie stormed the social club. Once inside, he argued with the Italians before drawing his gun and firing in the club. Although no-one was wounded, his point had been made. The Kray twins were not to be trifled with. As Ronnie commented himself in later years "we weren't playing kids games anymore."

The twins began to transition into more serious crime. The Regal started to be used as a gang headquarters as well as a business and party zone. They removed the cavalcade of tearaways and hangers on that had been frequenting the club and replaced them with more ambitious criminals. People who wanted to take their life of crime seriously. They called themselves 'The Firm' and they became a who's who of the criminal underworld in London. One man who, notably, never managed to join the inner circle of The Firm was Jack 'the Hat' McVitie. Even though the twins didn't know it, he would go on to play a very big part in their lives.

The twins began to make an incredible amount of money and their turf covered a significant area of the East End of London. With the majority of the businesses, both legal and otherwise, paying a percentage of their earnings to the Kray twins, they could afford to live a lifestyle befitting of two successful gangsters.

It was during 1956 that Ronnie's unhinged behavior and penchant for violence first became a serious problem for the twins in a business sense. A car dealer who had paid protection from the twins had trouble with a disgruntled customer. The customer was threatening to bring friends with him to extract a refund from the dealer. Ronnie dealt with the issue by shooting the disgruntled customer in the leg when he returned to the car dealer.

This lead to the victim of the shooting identifying Ronnie as the shooter, but when the police arrested him, he swore blind that he was Reggie and even had identification to prove it. Whether it was Ronnie or Reggie who was arrested is still a mystery to this day, but whoever the shooter was had

Reggie's driving license and was released without charge.

While all of this was happening, a fixer was employed to make sure that the problem went away. All people involved were made to promise their silence and the victim of the shooting was financially remunerated for his troubles.

This served only to add to Ronnie's sense of invulnerability that he had gained from his Mother's smothering as a child. It became a bone of contention between the twins; Ronnie constantly bragging of being untouchable annoyed Reggie as he felt angered that he had to clean up Ronnie's mess. He told him "you shoot a man, and then leave me to clean up the mess. One day you'll get us hanged."

The twins' reputation as men who could sort out trouble was eventually what lead them to their first real bump in the road as criminals, and first shed a real light on Ronnie's mental health issues. A friend of the Kray twins, Billie Jones, had taken over a club that had a lot of issues with trouble, a situation that mirrored their own takeover of The Regal. The owner couldn't handle all of the trouble, especially as it brought the interest of the police down on the club. An associate of Jones and the Krays, Bobby Ramsay, suggested that the twins come on board as partners. Although it would end up being a decision that would cost Ronnie dearly, they were happy to do so as in their eyes it was another revenue stream. A revenue stream that was, most importantly, a legitimate business.

Not long after this business arrangement, Billie Jones found himself involved in a dispute with a member of a gang from the docks. The gangs from the docks always had issues with the gangs from the rest of the East End of London. They were tough, and had easy access to items that they could steal coming through the dock. Jones came off worse in a fight with a gang member, this prompted Ramsay to get involved. As the altercations escalated, Ramsay ended up being beaten quite severely. This prompted Ronnie and Reggie to feel as though they had to become involved, after all, they were business partners of the two men.

Ronnie and Reggie set up members of the gang, targeting them while they were drinking in a pub. Unfortunately for the twins, details of their plan had got out to the gang. They all ran out of the back of the pub as the twins entered. Only one man failed to escape: Terry Martin. Bobby Ramsay identified Terry Martin as one of the men who had beaten him. He was then taken outside and almost beaten to death.

The twins were stopped that same night by a passing police car. Ronnie and Reggie were tried with GBH and Ronnie had an additional charge of carrying a firearm. Reggie managed to dodge the charges, but Ronnie was not so lucky and ended up being sent to jail for three years.

While Ronnie served his sentence, the fortunes of the twins could not have been more different. Reggie managed to grow their empire, both criminal and legitimate. The twins owned at least thirty businesses in the East End of London by the time Ronnie was finally out of prison.

Ronnie had always been the dominant twin, even though Reggie had a more keen business sense. Their differences had often cost them financially; however, now that Ronnie was in jail, Reggie could make more sound business decisions, allowing their empire to continue growing.

The Regency was scheduled to be knocked down by powers outside of the Krays' influence, so Reggie decided to move the location of their headquarters elsewhere. He settled on an abandoned shop. The Firm organized the decorating and within four months of Ronnie being sent to jail, Reggie opened his new club, named with his brother in mind, The Double R.

It attracted all manner of celebrities and rich clientele. Reggie finally felt he had made it. He wasn't just mingling with celebrities, he was now one himself. Charlie, the twins' brother, came back into his life. He made suggestions for Reggie to extend his legitimate business interests. Reggie was all too happy to take these on board and the Kray Empire continued to grow.

Ronnie however suffered from much worse fortune. While in jail his mental health deteriorated at an alarming rate. He began to worry he was being targeted by unknown people. These delusions only intensified when he was moved to a prison on the Isle of Wight, where no-one knew of his status and influence. The guards became worried for his well-being and kept watch over him to ensure he wouldn't hurt himself. This only made Ronnie more nervous.

He was diagnosed as suffering from 'prison psychosis', which at the time covered any kind of mental illness brought on by being locked up. He was medicated and seemed to be recovering, until he heard the news of the death of his Aunt Rose. She died on Christmas day 1957, Ronnie found out on the 27th. He became manic and had to be placed in a strait-jacket to stop him from hurting himself. On the 28th of December, his mother Violet received a telegram from the prison: "Your son Ronald Kray is certified insane."

Ronnie was diagnosed with schizophrenia, although the authorities were not completely correct with the diagnosis, after being transferred to a lunatic asylum in Surrey named Long Grove Hospital. While here, doctors noticed an improvement in Ronnie's condition, and the decision was made that he should stay at Long Grove rather than be transferred back to prison.

Ronnie was not happy with this decision and, by the end of May that year, he was desperate to escape. Luckily, Reggie had the perfect plan. On an allotted visiting day, the twins switched places. When the staff at Long Grove was finally aware about what had happened, it was too late; Ronnie was long gone. It was during Ronnie's premature freedom that Reggie realized he had made a big mistake.

The plan was for Ronnie to stay hidden for six weeks, because anyone who was outside for that long had to be reclassified, then Ronnie would hand himself over, be classified as sane and then serve the last of his term in regular prison. However, Ronnie couldn't handle this. He was becoming more and more paranoid by the day. He offered to kill the troublesome neighbor of the farmer whose land he was hiding on. He was taken back to the East End by Reggie and a doctor was brought in to help him settle. Ronnie was surviving on two bottles of gin and multiple tranquilizers a day. He was a mess.

Finally, Reggie realized his error of judgement. Even though the twins had a code of silence, Reggie broke that code in order to help his brother. He phoned Scotland Yard and they arranged to pick up Ronnie the next morning at 2am. Ronnie left with the police without even looking at his family. Reggie was distraught.

In a strange twist of fate, Ronnie only spent two more weeks at Long Grove. He was diagnosed fit to finish his sentence and finally in 1959 he was released from prison. The Krays were back together, but Ronnie was different and it spelled the start of their eventual downfall.

After Ronnie's release from prison, the difference in him was astounding. Not just in his attitude - he'd always been the more violent and short tempered of the pair - it was also clear from his appearance. His eyes were tighter, his jaw line had altered. He looked and acted, according to one report, like 'a demon'. He wasn't the intimidating man he used to be. Ronnie soon started to cause trouble for Reggie. It was most apparent when he threatened violence and demanded protection money from a gambling den that Reggie already owned.

The former financial security that Reggie had created was slowly becoming smaller and smaller. Their business interests barely covered their expenses. For all of Reggie's business acumen, Ronnie was equally as violent. It didn't help the business aspect of the Krays' empire. It did, however, make sure that they stayed just as feared as ever.

Ronnie was dragging the twins down, but it was Reggie who made the next mistake. The twins made friends with a car dealer named Daniel Shay. Shay attempted to extort a local shopkeeper with the twins in tow. When the trio left, the shopkeeper called the police. When Shay and Reggie went back to collect the money, they were both arrested. Shay was sentenced to three years in jail and Ronnie eighteen months.

This gave Ronnie exactly what he longed for. He no longer had Reggie to curtail his more violent plans. He could finally do what he always wanted. He could go to war. He had already acquired the nickname Colonel, now he finally had a war to fight, and troops to command.

He started by targeting Peter Rachman. Rachman was a slum lord in Notting Hill, which was not the elite metropolitan area it is known as today. Rachman resisted paying protection money, but knew that he would never get out from under Ronnie's protection racket if he started paying. He needed something else, and he found it when the government made the decision to legalise gambling.

Rachman knew Stefan De Faye, who owned Esmerelda's Barn which was in a very upmarket area of London (not far from Buckingham Palace). A meeting was set up, which Reggie was able to attend as he was out on bail, and the twins were joined by their friend Leslie Payne. De Faye agreed to sell his shareholder in the club but stay on as an executive and manager to run the club.

The club was an absolute gold mine for the twins. They made almost £100,000 a year from their shareholding in the club, which, in the early 1960s, was an incredible sum of money (it would be the equivalent of earning £1.6 million in 2017 as a frame of reference).

Unfortunately for Reggie, his appeal failed and he was sent back to prison just after Christmas that year. It was a bad thing for Ronnie too, as he soon began to lose control of his finances and his behavior. He had gained a taste for the high life from being a regular socialite. Just as Reggie had when he opened the Double R, Ronnie started associating with celebrities. He also made a number of bad choices that impacted Esmerelda's Barn.

Ronnie took huge markers that bounced. The manager of Esmerelda's Barn offered Ronnie £1000 a week just to stay away from the club. Ronnie refused; he didn't care about the money. He loved the lifestyle. He used his money and fame to sleep with young men, of any creed or color, Ronnie was proud that he was without prejudice. Regardless, he still craved violence. A clairvoyant told him that he was a reincarnation of Atilla the Hun and he would achieve greatness through violence and then die young. Ronnie's violent tendencies may have calmed down, but they didn't go away.

The influence of Leslie Payne caused the business interests of the twins to explode beyond their wildest dreams. They used what they called the "long firm" fraud. They would open a business and run it by the book. When they had the trust of suppliers they would place large orders on credit, sell the items at any price and then the business would vanish without a trace, leaving creditors wondering what had happened.

Payne set up a legitimate business operation with an accountant to cover their shady domestic and international deals. It was around this time that Ronnie thought he had found what would be his ticket to immortality.

He met Ernest Shinwell, the son of a famous politician. Shinwell was involved in building a village in Nigeria. Ronnie saw this as the act of philanthropy that would catapult him to greatness. There was a lot of interest from the Nigerian government but their issue was financing.

The Kray twins decided to invest their own money in the project. Unfortunately, there were some less-than-scrupulous people involved in the deal. Payne was detained in Nigeria and the twins had to bail him out. Ronnie was crushed at losing his opportunity for immortality. His rage began to become uncontrollable.

He started thinking of new ways to punish people who crossed The Firm, to the point that he openly mentioned castrating people. Reggie struggled to control Ronnie's violent urges. A boxer had his face slashed by Ronnie which resulted in the boxer requiring over 70 stitches, all stemming from the Nigerian deal collapsing.

Part 2 – Murders and Victims

The man, who was involved with the first meeting between Ronnie and Lord Boothby, Leslie Holt, died under very strange circumstances. It is rumored to have been one of the Kray Twins first murders, but is by no means confirmed. Surprisingly, for two with such a violent career and how quickly they climbed the ladder of crime, Ronnie and Reggie were only ever convicted of two murders.

The first murder that it is known they committed was that of George Cornell. Despite all of Ronnie's anger issues around this time; it wasn't this that caused the murder of George Cornell. The cause was the rumblings of a gang war between The Krays and a gang south of the River Thames, The Richardsons.

When a known Richardson associate "Mad" Frankie Fraser worked his way into taking some gambling machines that the Krays owned, Ronnie was not happy. As a response they tried to take a slice of an extortion racket that the Richardson's were running at Heathrow car park. When this didn't happen, they were waiting for a moment for revenge, but in the end it wasn't even all of this that caused them to kill George Cornell.

There was already heat between the twins and George Cornell after he had told the twins to back off over the extortion racket, Cornell a former member of The Firm, had switched sides when he got married, was a large intimidating man. Not afraid of anyone or of handling any business he needed to, in any way.

He was drinking in a club named Mr. Smith's on March 8th 1966. He was with other members of the Richardson gang; Frankie Fraser, Harry Rawlings, Ron Jeffries, Jimmy Moody and their boss Eddie Richardson. The club was owned by two men from Manchester and the Richardsons handled both club security and the gambling machines on the premises.

The club didn't just hold drinkers from one gang. It was host to a number of gangs from the south of London. On this particular night there was a gang of men drinking there that included Richard Hart, a cousin of the Kray twins. The trouble which later ensued that night was not related to the gangs being rivals, however. Billy Hayward, a man drinking with Richard Hart had been having an extramarital affair with the mechanic for the Richardson gang. Fearing retribution for his indiscretions, he began shooting at the men from the Richardson gang on the other side of the pub.

Harry Rawlings was shot through the shoulder, Frankie Fraser and Eddie Richardson were both wounded by bullets and Richard Hart was shot dead. This shoot-out ultimately lead to the breakup of the

Richardson gang, as many of the men involved were arrested and sent to prison.

Even though the police arrested most of the people involved in the shoot-out, the Kray twins took the death of their cousin, Richard Hart, as a personal insult. The rumors that were flying around the East End of London were that George Cornell was the man who fired the shot that killed Richard Hart. Ronnie and Reggie wanted revenge and they didn't have to wait long to get it.

The very next day, George Cornell was drinking in a pub named The Blind Beggar. Ronnie, Reggie and The Firm were in a pub named The Lion not far away. An unknown assailant phoned The Lion and informed the twins of Cornell's whereabouts. The twins took two of The Firm with them and made their way to The Blind Beggar to confront George Cornell. The two men were John Dickson and Ian Barrie – their driver. They drove to the pub and pulled up right outside.

As Ronnie and Ian Barrie walked into the pub, George Cornell gave them a submissive glance and remarked with a sarcastic snarl "Well, look who's here now". Ronnie walked right up to the bar where Cornell was sat, pulled out his gun and shot him in the head three times. Ian Barrie fired his gun into the ceiling as the bar staff and customers all ducked for cover. Cornell collapsed and hit a pillar; one of the bullets hit the jukebox, forcing it to stick on the track that was playing. Ironically, the song was titled "The

Sun Ain't Gonna Shine Anymore". It didn't for George Cornell.

While the initial motivation for the murder of George Cornell was the death of Richard Hart, it was also rooted in Ronnie and Reggie needing to keep control of The Firm. If they hadn't taken action after the death of one of theirs at the hand of another gang, then they would have looked weak and may have lost control of their own. While the rumors did say that Cornell was the one that shot Richard Hart, it was also a matter of Cornell being the only one who wasn't in jail. Added to all of these factors that Cornell had been bad mouthing the Krays, it could have been any one of these factors that made them take the decision to shoot George

Cornell, or was most likely the combination of all of them.

Scotland Yard assigned the case of finding Cornell's killer to Superintendent Butler, but was hindered from the start. All witnesses to the crime denied having seen anything, with the barmaid even going as far as being unable to identify Ronnie in a line up. Ronnie went free but he wasn't as confident as he had been when he had escaped arrest. Rumors of fresh evidence being found scared the twins and they ran off to Morocco until they were thrown out by the chief of police for being undesirable aliens.

Although they had gotten away with the first murder they committed, the second one was the one that proved to be their undoing.

After the killing of Cornell, Reggie had been trying to reconcile with his wife Frances. They booked a holiday together in Ibiza, but tragically, Frances committed suicide shortly after. Now it was Reggie's turn to descend into a pit of depression and poor mental health. He began drinking heavily and started to make rash, violent decisions that were completely different to his usual cool demeanor. Reggie became like Ronnie; twisted, mean and very dangerous.

He shot two people, albeit only wounding them. He sliced a man's face open with a knife and two members of The Firm vanished while a third who tried to leave was left a funeral wreath on his front door. While there is no concrete evidence about what happened to the two members of The

Firm who disappeared, Reggie Kray claimed on his deathbed that he had been denied parole because of his involvement in another killing in addition to what he had been arrested for. This is thought to be "Mad" Teddy Smith, although it has never been proven.

Ronnie always wondered why his brother didn't seem to have it in him to kill someone. Ronnie spent a lot of time bragging about how he had shot George Cornell and got away with it. Reggie always seemed to stop short of killing, and Ronnie never understood why. When Reggie finally did decide to cross the line and kill someone, it was crossing that line that was finally the undoing of the Kray twin's empire.

Before they got to the man that proved to be their undoing, they sprung an old prison friend from jail with the intention of gaining media attention for his case and hopefully getting it reinvestigated. The man was Frank Mitchell "The Mad Axeman" who had broken into an old couple's home and held them up with an axe. He was a large man and had a history of mental illness. He was not unlike Ronnie in this respect. After he was broken out of prison the aim was for Mitchell to give himself up to the police once media attention had been gained. Unfortunately, it never got to that stage.

In late December 1966, Frank Mitchell was killed. The exact details of the murder are unreliable, but Freddie Foreman admitted in his autobiography that he had shot Mitchell.

Their reasoning behind shooting Mitchell was that he had become too much of a problem. They couldn't handle his short temper or his refusal to give himself up.

It was decided that Mitchell had to be taken care of before the twins were implicated in his escape from prison. Albert Donoghue told Mitchell he was being moved to a safe house in the countryside, but once he got Mitchell in the back of his van Foreman and another man shot him to death. According to Foreman they dumped his body in the English Channel, but was never recovered.

The twins were eventually charged with the murder of Mitchell, but there was not enough evidence to prove that they either had anything to do with it, or that they carried it out themselves. The Mitchell situation brought more attention to the twins, but it wasn't the final nail in their careers as criminals, that elusive honor goes to the decision to murder Jack "The Hat" McVitie.

Jack "The Hat" McVitie was an associate of The Firm, although he was not a fully-fledged member. He was nicknamed "The Hat" because he reportedly never removed the hat he used to hide his bald patch (according to some reports, even when he took a bath). He was different to the other members because he had no real respect for Ronnie or Reggie, and he certainly didn't fear them. He regularly carried out jobs for them, without becoming part of the inner circle.

It first became apparent that his uses might not outweigh the problems he created when he reneged on a deal to kill the twins' former business manager Leslie Payne. The twins were worried that Payne was going to talk to the police to avoid a charge hanging over his head. Ronnie paid McVitie one hundred pounds to kill Payne, with the promise of a further four hundred to be paid once the job was done. Jack McVitie didn't do the job, and not only did he not do it, but he also refused to pay back the deposit Ronnie had given him in advance. Ronnie was not happy about this, and he marked it in his mental scorecard.

The next time McVitie had a mark against him was after a day of drinking. McVitie stumbled into the 211 Club, which happened to be owned by an associate of the Krays, Billy Foreman. While in the 211 Club, McVitie threatened to wreck the whole place. This again angered Ronnie and pushed him closer to taking action against him.

Jack McVitie's third and final strike came when he threatened to owners of The Regency Club with a sawn-off shotgun. John and Tony Barrie, the owners, were both associates of the twins. This caused not only Ronnie to be past the point of no return, but even Reggie too. Even though Reggie was still in his downward spiral at this point, he was still more measured than Ronnie and he also found McVitie's actions a step too far. He knew something had to be done before he did some real damage, either to their earnings or to their reputations.

They decided to set a trap for Jack The Hat. On October 28th, 1967 the twins were drinking at The Carpenter's Arms with a number of their associates. A rumor among the local people was that a party was going to be happening later in the evening at a house owned by a woman named Carol Skinner, or "Blonde Carol". As luck would have it she also lived with a man who worked for the Kray twins.

While in The Carpenter's Arms a member of The Firm, Tony Lambrianou, introduced the Krays to friends of theirs from Birmingham; twins named Tony Mills and Alan Mills. They just so happened to be good friends with McVitie. They met up with him and a Kray associate Ronnie Hart in The Regency, and when the men from Birmingham suggested an after-hours party, Jack The Hat was only too happy to agree.

The men got into a car and made their way to Blonde Carol's house where Reggie and Ronnie had been clearing guests away for around an hour. When they pulled up just before midnight, there was only two of Ronnie's lovers and a man named Ronnie Bender at the house. Ronnie Hart, the Mills twins and Jack McVitie entered the flat. As McVitie entered the room Reggie walked right up to him, pointed his gun at his head and fired. Almost like a precursor for things to come, the gun jammed. Ronnie began screaming in McVitie's face while his lovers and the Mills twins ran from the house. Reggie began pushing and shoving McVitie across the room. McVitie tried to escape from a window but Reggie pulled him back in.

Jack McVitie was now standing in the room, without his hat, sweating profusely and looked visibly afraid; the first time he had ever been afraid of the Krays, "Why are you doing this, Reg?" he asked. He didn't get an answer, Ronnie just kept screaming at Reggie to kill McVitie. Reggie complied with his brother, he grabbed a knife from Ronnie Bender and stabbed it into McVitie's face just below his eye, then stabbed him in the chest repeatedly. Finally he stuck the knife through McVitie's throat, pinning him to the floor. That final stab almost symbolizing the death of the Kray family as well as the literal death of Jack "The Hat" McVitie.

Finally dead, McVitie's body was wrapped in bedding and placed in Ronnie Bender's car. Tony Lambrianou drove it away, followed in another car by Ronnie Bender and Tony's brother Chris Lambrianou. Even though they were told to dump the body in the East End, they decided instead to dump it in Richardson turf to try and lay the blame at their feet. When the Krays found out, they became worried. They thought the blame may have been laid at the feet of their associate Billy Foreman rather than the Richardsons.

They phoned their brother Charlie who drove across London and made arrangements with Freddie Foreman, Billy's brother, and Ronnie Hart to have the body disposed of, and they did. Jack "The Hat"

McVitie's body has still not been found to this day.

After the murder Reggie Kray said "I did not regret it at the time and I don't regret it now. I have never felt a moment's regret." In hindsight, he should have. This murder was what finally stopped the Krays' reign of terror, and what caused them to spend almost all of the rest of their life in prison.

Part 3 - Accomplices

Part of Ronnie and Reggie's success as criminals was their associates, who they referred to as The Firm. When they first started out, they used a collection of waifs and strays to carry out their dirty work, but as the progressed up the ranks of crime, they more and more surrounded themselves with hardened criminals.

Using people more inclined to a life of crime yielded much more success for the twins. While The Firm was not always organized, Ronnie and Reggie knew they always had reliable people who would be willing to take on any task. The first of these men was Albert Donoghue.

Albert Donoghue was an integral part of the Kray's day to day lives. He was Ronnie Krays personal minder for a while. It could have all been so different though, as on one of their early meetings Albert said something out of turn and Reggie Kray shot him in the leg as a punishment. When Donoghue said nothing to the police about the shooting it earned him a place in The Firm.

Donoghue was a part of many of the Krays most famous exploits, including helping to keep Frank "The Mad Axeman" Mitchell placid by taking supplies to him. On the night that the Krays ordered Freddie Foreman to kill Mitchell, it was Donoghue who lured him into the van to get shot, and then Donoghue helped to keep the girl who had been staying with Mitchell placated by spending the night with her.

Donoghue eventually had a big part in the downfall of the Kray twins, when he refused to take the fall for the murder of Mitchell. He thought that he was to be next and he testified in court against the twins when they finally went a step too far.

Ian Barrie was another member of The Firm who played an important role in both the Krays day to day life, but also their downfall. A tough man from Glasgow, Ian Barrie was the man that Ronnie Kray used as his right hand man when he murdered George Cornell. Ian was loyal and worked hard for the Krays, usually the man that Ronnie would turn to the most, after Reggie of course.

Ian Barrie not only accompanied Ronnie Kray into the pub when he shot George Cornell, but he also ensured that no-one did anything that might cause them trouble when he fired his warning shots. The other member of The Firm to accompany Ronnie on the murder of George Cornell was "Scotch" Jack Dickson.

Jack Dickson usually worked as a driver for the Krays. He was a loyal soldier and did whatever was needed to keep their empire ticking over. However, Jack's loyally was tested towards the end of his relationship with the Krays, when he found out that they intended to persuade him to take the fall for the murder of George Cornell. Jack later testified against them in court.

While Ian Barrie never turned against the twins, he did do jail time for his involvement in the killing of Cornell. After his release from jail in the 1980s, Ian Barrie disappeared. No-one knows to this day what happened to him or even if he is still alive.

Pat Connolly, Big Tommy Brown, Billy Donovan, Connie Whitehead, John Barry, Sammy Lederman, Dave Simmonds and Nobby Clark were all members of The Firm who first became part of the group when the Krays bought their first club The Regal. It was during this time that the first transition from young, tough children being the main part of the Kray gang to tough, criminal men being the main aspect.

John Barry, in addition to being a member of The Firm also owned The Regency club with his brother. They were paying protection money to the Krays, who also acted as silent partners in the running of the club. It was at The Regency that Jack McVitie put one of the nails into his coffin after his numerous antics, including threatening to shoot a man, stabbing someone and wiping the knife on a woman's dress and threatening to shoot both Barry brothers. This caused John Barry to complain to the Krays about the actions of McVitie.

These men all formed the basis of the muscle of the Kray gang. Carrying out all manner of extortion and intimidation to ensure that the Krays rose to the top of the pyramid of the gangs in the East End of London. Many of them started after leaving jail or if they were just down on their luck. The Krays believed in helping people to get on their feet. They believed that this kind of criminal philanthropy would result in greater loyalty from their underlings.

Chris and Tony Lambrianou were two brothers who were part of The Firm. They were two of the Krays most trusted and loyal members, and are most well known for their part in the murder of Jack "The Hat" McVitie. They played an integral part in getting McVitie to move on to the house of Carol Skinner, using their friends the Mills twins who were in turn friends with McVitie.

In addition, they were in attendance when the murder took place, and then helped with the moving of the body.

The Lambrianou brothers ended up being two of the most loyal members of The Firm, as they didn't testify in court against the Krays when they were finally caught out and charged. They also served 15 years each for their part in the murder of Jack McVitie.

Ronnie Bender worked as a driver for the Krays. Another loyal member of The Firm, he never betrayed their confidence. He worked as a driver for them most commonly, and was involved in the disposal of McVitie's body. He attempted to leave the body on a railway line so that a train would destroy it, but was unable to fit the body in the boot of his car and so had to drive McVitie's car with the body on the back seat. He didn't testify against them in court, maintaining his loyalty to the twins, and ended up serving a life sentence for his involvement in the murder of McVitie.

Part 4 – Arrest & Evidence

The Krays criminal empire was far reaching across the majority of the East End of London by 1967. They hadn't paid much thought to the interest in them from Scotland Yard, but it was about to become a very serious issue, an issue that would end their careers as criminals, and their lives as free men.

After being promoted to the "murder squad", Detective Superintendent Leonard "Nipper" Read was given the task of bringing the Krays to justice. Having tried in the early 60s, but coming up against political opposition and the famous East End silence, Read was more than familiar with the illegal activities of the Kray twins.

Leonard Read was the perfect candidate to go after Ronnie and Reggie. He had been promoted to Detective Inspector at a very young age of 36 and had done so with his talent and hard work, rather than political machinations. By the time he was 43 he had been promoted to Detective Superintendent and was officially recognized as one of the top 12 detectives in the whole of England. This time, he would not be denied his convictions.

He had noticed that Scotland Yard didn't seem to spend much time or effort in attempting to bring down the Kray twins. It infuriated him that the top people had almost given up on ever stopping them. Whether that was due to their skills at avoiding the law or due to greased palms is unknown. He set about building his team to bring them down.

By mid-1967 he had brought in John du Rose, head of the Murder Squad, Superintendent Harry Mooney, Superintendent Don Adams, and Chief-Inspector Frank Cater. These men became the basis of the squad to apprehend the Krays. With additional fifteen staff members they were well manned and had all of the resources they needed to finally bring an end to Kray twins reign as the heads of The Firm.

Read called a meeting of his team, he told them that they would have a deadline on their investigation of three months. Read was slightly optimistic on this deadline as it would take slightly longer than that to finally take the twins down. Their first port of call was to try to gather information from the people of the East End. It didn't garner any useful results. The code of silence prevailed and the Kray squad had to try a change of tack.

In the midst of all of this, Leonard Read had been ensuring that his men had been training for the possibility of a physical confrontation with the Kray gang. He had been making his men practice with the use of a handgun. Just like is the case now, the English police didn't regularly use handguns. He wanted to make sure that if it came down to a fire fight his men would not be outclassed by the Kray gang who were all proficient in the use of firearms. Additionally, they had to make sure that they changed their travel routes daily and their family members were prepared for if anything untoward happened.

Read's first port of call was a man named Alan Bruce Cooper. Cooper was being used as a source from within Scotland Yard and had employed a man named Paul Elvey, who was involved in three failed attempts at murder. When he was arrested and his link to Cooper revealed, Read found out about him being a high level source and attempted to use him as bait. Unfortunately the Krays didn't take the bait, and Read had to go back to the drawing board for a new plan.

Read made a choice that he would not be able to get the Kray twins on their current activity, and instead would have to focus on their past indiscretions. Read decided that the best form of attack would be to isolate weak links in The Firm. Read got thirty names and wrote them down in a black notebook. He called this his "delightful index".

Read and du Rose started investigating the legitimate businesses under the Krays' empire; mainly nightclubs and betting shops which acted as fronts for their illegal activities and places where they could launder money. It was at this point that the Kray squad realized that they would have to both approach and rely on in court, criminals, to get the evidence and testimony they would need to send the Kray twins to jail. The police higher ups were initially resistant to this approach.

Read and du Rose became involved in a heated discussion with the top brass at Scotland Yard, including the police lawyers, but eventually managed to convince them that the testimony of criminals would be important in the case. At first they had very little luck, with one man telling them "I hate the sight of blood, especially my own."

Finally, Read and his team had a breakthrough. Leslie Payne got word to Read. He wanted to talk. Payne had been aware of the plan for Jack "The Hat" McVitie to murder him. He was also aware of the fact that McVitie had vanished after he had failed to kill him. Payne knew that he had to protect himself from the Krays, and knew that the underworld wouldn't be willing to help him. He knew he had to turn to the law, and so he did.

After Read got in touch with him, he was taken to a hotel in Marylebone. Here Payne stayed for three weeks, telling Read and his team everything that he could remember. In all he filled over two hundred pages of notes about the twins illegal activities. From violence and racketeering to their long term frauds, Leslie Payne detailed everything that he knew. By Christmas 1967 Nipper Read had a large database of information about the Kray twins and their illegal empire, and now all he needed was proof and witnesses to finally take them down for good.

By January 1968 Read and the rest of his team were tirelessly chasing down the leads that Leslie Payne had given them. The investigation took them across all of Europe and even as far as the United States at one point. Nipper Read and his team were working twenty four hours a day, seven days a week. They left no stone unturned in their pursuit of Ronnie and Reggie Kray.

Ronnie and Reggie were keeping a low profile during this time. Their own sources had told them that the police had begun to gather evidence against them. While they were not worried, they also didn't know how much information that the police actually had on them. Bizarrely, Ronnie bought himself a python at this point, going so far as to name it Read.

It was around this time that Ronnie bought a Victorian mansion and achieved a lifelong dream of becoming a country squire. It was here that the twins began to spend most of their time. While their criminal earnings were severely limited by the increased police scrutiny, they were still working on their plans, although now they were obviously no longer using Leslie Payne as their business manager.

During April Ronnie travelled to New York. There, he met up with a selection of gamblers, boxers and small time criminals. Although Ronnie did meet with two of the Gallo brothers - a crime family who were waging a war with the New York mafia - he didn't meet with anyone of real importance, and no serious plans were made on his trip.

Alan Cooper was the man they were using at this time as their business manager. They were completely unaware that Cooper was not only informing for Scotland Yard but was also working for the US treasury after he had been caught on a gold smuggling trip.

All of this information was not known by the Krays, so when Ronnie planned with Cooper to restructure the way The Firm worked, mainly to be more in line with how the American mafia was, he didn't know that this information was being passed on to Scotland Yard. It was at this time that Ronnie decided to assassinate certain important people in order to gain more respect from the American crime families and possibly build up a better working relationship.

He instructed Alan Cooper to sort out the supplies needed for a car bomb, as he felt this way would be the most impressive. Cooper used Paul Elvey for the task of procuring the explosives, but Elvey was arrested on his way back to London. During interrogation, he gave up Cooper and it was at this point that Nipper Read found out about Cooper being an informant for Scotland Yard. It was now that Read had a difficult choice to make: charge him as an accessory, or release him and use him as a witness. Read went with the latter.

On May 8th Read brought his team together for one last meeting before they made their move. The plan was to strike first thing in the morning on May 9th. Armed officers were to arrest the twins and twenty four members of The Firm all at the same time. It had to happen simultaneously at twenty four different addresses to ensure that no-one could tell the others about the operation.

The need for all people to be arrested at once was to ensure that potential witnesses couldn't be coerced. As this was the way the Krays had managed to get out of all previous arrests, it was a very real possibility that they would use this tactic again.

Once all the teams were ready they began the operation. The twins were both with lovers when their door was smashed in. Ronnie with a young boy and Reggie with a young girl. Neither had any idea what was going on when they were arrested. Luckily for the police, the handgun training hadn't been needed.

All in all, only two of The Firm had managed to avoid capture: Ian Barrie and Ronnie Hart. It was feared that the case would fall apart as witnesses became aware that they may be targets, but the pair were quickly apprehended and the case went ahead.

On July 6th the twins had their preliminary hearing. It was here that Ronnie and Reggie first realized just how much trouble they were actually in. A member of their crew, Billy Exley, arrived to give evidence against the Krays. He knew a lot of their inner secrets and information on their long term frauds. Billy being there was a bad sign for Ronnie and Reggie. Added to this the barmaid from the night George Cornell was killed agreed to be a witness. Although she had been unable to identify Ronnie in a line up at the time, the promise of police protection and a new identity she was more than happy to point out Ronnie Kray and Ian Barrie as the two men who had entered The Blind Beggar pub on the night George Cornell was murdered.

The Krays were kept on remand until the actual trial, and Read was constantly worried that they would be able to get to witnesses. After eight months on remand, the trial began in January 1969.

The biggest surprise and possibly the most hurtful betrayal from all of The Firm was that of Ronnie Hart. Ronnie Hart was the twin's cousin, and had been involved in many of their illegal activities for a long time, most notably the slaying of Jack "The Hat" McVitie. The betrayal by Hart cut the twins deep, and had a lasting effect on Ronnie Hart too. He later attempted to commit suicide, although failed. After this, he immigrated to Australia.

Even though Ronnie and Reggie Kray had been running their criminal empire for over a decade, they were only tried for the murders of George Cornell and Jack McVitie. This was partly down to their skills at hiding their tracks and the code of silence that was prevalent throughout the East End of London. The trial lasted for two months, and on the 8th March 1969 the Kray twins were sentenced to life in prison, with the judge recommending that they serve no less than thirty years in prison.

Other members of The Firm that were sentenced included their brother Charlie, who gotten years for accessory to the murder of Jack Mcvitie. Ian Barrie received a life sentence for his part in the Cornell murder. Four other members of The Firm, including the Lambrianou brothers, Ronnie Bender and Albert Donoghue, were also sentenced at the same time as the Krays.

Finally, after months of work, Read had caught his men. The Krays' reign of terror over the East End of London was over. Ronnie and Reggie had run a successful if disorganized empire for more than ten years and in the end were only convicted of two murders between them. This was a much more surprising incident than the fact that their career as criminals were finally at an end.

Part 5 - Legacy

While the Kray twins have had a lasting legacy and effect on popular culture in the world, and England especially, their legacy is especially felt in the East End of London. It is still a hotbed of crime to this day. Almost as soon as the Krays were jailed more gangs popped up to take their place.

Detective Sergeant Harry Challenor of the Flying Squad, the division of the police that the television series "The Sweeney" was based on, once commented:

"Fighting crime in London was like trying to swim against a tide of sewage; you made two strokes forward and were swept back three. For every villain you put behind bars there were always two more to take their place."

Harry Challenor was right, criminals didn't see their rivals being arrested as a deterrent, and they saw it as an opportunity. The more criminals that were locked up, the more new ones sprouted up to take their place. The East End of London is seemingly destined to always be a place that attracts opportunistic villains who want to make their fortune off the hard work of others.

Almost as soon as the Krays were put away, The Dixons took on their business interests. When The Dixons were gone, The Tibbs came and went. Bertie Small, The Arif Family, The Legal and General Gang, the

Knight Family, the list could go on forever. And unfortunately, it seems that it will.

Not only did new gangs pop up constantly, but two of the men who were most responsible for bringing down the Kray twins, John du Rose and Leonard "Nipper" Read fell out of the picture. John du Rose, who became known as "Four Day Johnny" due to how fast he solved his cases, retired from Scotland Yard and Read moved north to become the Deputy Chief Constable of Nottingham police. These two men not only had a huge part to play in the Krays arrest and conviction, but they also had an aura that seemed to make criminals keep a lower profile. With them out of the picture, the criminals became a lot braver and a lot more brazen.

This is not to say that crime had never been an issue in the East End, it had always had a crime problem long before the Kray twins. What the Kray twins did was glamourize it; normalize it. People like to romanticize about their era. In the East End, it is common to hear people comment how certain crimes, like muggings of the elderly, wouldn't have happened in Ron and Reg's day. It doesn't occur to them that this normalization of their criminal activities is partly what encourages the modern day criminal to follow this path.

Part of the romanticizing of the criminal lifestyle and the assertion that things were better than is also perpetuated by criminals of the time, like Tony Lambrianou who said:

"The East End was a hard place; it became famous for turning out gangsters. There was a better class of criminal in those days, there were rules you lived by, and if you broke them, you paid the price. Back when I was doing it, the code was this: You don't grass on your own mates ever. You respect women. You never steal off your own. The violence was among ourselves, or between us and people who knew our rules. If anyone was dealing with us, they were shady to begin with and they knew the score. The streets were safer when we was around, because no one in their right mind would come into our area and commit crimes. People don't respect life like we used to, or even respect themselves. I mean look how people dress. We may have been villains, but we always looked sharp."

The last line the most telling of all, as though being well dressed excused their behavior.

Ronnie and Reggie Kray appearing with celebrities and being well known even by the general public in England was one of the first examples of criminals using the newspapers and media to legitimize what they did. Not only this, but they portrayed themselves as legitimate businessmen, so when the police did come down on them, they found it easy to play the victims.

Ronnie and Reggie Kray are an anomaly in this world. They did terrible things to a lot of people, but they are still spoken about with great fondness. Part of this is down to the influence of their Mother. She instilled the trait of helping those down on their luck.

Ronnie especially could not help himself when it came to helping those less fortunate, and he especially liked to help people just released from prison. These traits made a lot of people forget their indiscretions and lead to them being falsely remembered as heroes of the East End, rather than the vicious, ruthless and cruel criminals that they really were.

One of the biggest examples of this fondness in the East End came in 1995 when Ronnie Kray died. On March 17th of 1995 Ronnie Kray suffered a heart attack. Most likely caused by years of excessive smoking, Ronnie had smoked at least 100 cigarettes every day of his adult life, not to mention spent much of his time in smoky clubs. Reggie and the twins elder brother Charlie sorted the funeral between them and arranged it for the 29th March.

On Wednesday 29th March 1995 Ronnie Kray's funeral was held at St Mathews in Bethnal Green and was buried at Chingford Cemetery, which was six miles away. This cemetery was chosen because the twins Father, Mother and Reggie's wife Frances were all buried there. No expense was spared for the funeral and it cost £10,000. Thousands of people lined the streets from St Mathews in Bethnal Green, for the whole six miles to the cemetery.

The fact that all these people lined the streets, over twenty five years after the twins arrest and incarceration, shows the legacy of the Kray twins as well loved figures. In addition to this their funeral was attended by many gangsters from the era of the Krays, Frankie Fraser, Freddie Foreman, Johnny Nash and Teddy Dennis were all there, showing the respect the Krays held in the underworld, even almost 30 years after their involvement in it.

Another example of their lasting legacy was the death of their brother Charlie. On April 19th 2000, Charlie's funeral was held. Much like Ronnie's, thousands of people lined the streets. At 11am, Reggie Kray arrived at the funeral, handcuffed to a police officer; he was greeted by cheers and applause. Cheers and applause as though he was a war hero or film star, not a former criminal who had spent the previous thirty one years in jail.

On October 1st, Reggie Kray died of bladder cancer. His funeral was the biggest of them all. Police from six districts were called in to help control the crowd along the nine miles of road for the funeral procession. Ronnie had married in prison, and his wife Roberta threw a red rose into his grave; the same grave Ronnie had been buried in. The Krays had finally had their last influence on the East End, but as is apparent to this day their legacy was far from over.

The Krays legacy didn't just fall on the East End. They used their fame to sell books. The first book they wrote they wrote together and was released in 1988. Although the twins were credited as writers of the book, thirteen of the chapters were written by their ghostwriter Fred Dinenage. The second book, Born Fighter, written solely by Reggie Kray.

Born Fighter was written without the aid of a ghostwriter and tells Reggie's story of what happened while he and Ronnie ran their criminal empire. Released in 1990, it was very successful and brought the story of the Krays to a whole new generation of people. Helping to keep them in the public eye and making sure that their constant campaigning for release wasn't forgotten about.

Two years before he died, Ronnie released another book entitled My Story. Written as a sequel to the joint autobiography that he and Reggie had released in 1988, My Story told the story of many of his and Reggie's criminal activities as well as giving an insight into Ronnie's battle with mental health. It showed a slightly more sympathetic side to Ronnie Kray; one where he talked about being bisexual, how he hated being in Broadmoor and, although he didn't say it explicitly, his lack of understanding of his own mental illness.

The final book released by either of the Kray twins was entitled A Way of Life: Over Thirty Years of Blood, Sweat and Tears in the year 2000 and was written entirely by Reggie. This book was a move away from talking about their criminal career and spoke at length about Reggie's time behind bars. By its time of release, Reggie had spent almost half of his life in jail in total and not only did he feel like he had served his punishment, but his repeated requests for release had all been turned down. It wasn't until he was diagnosed with terminal cancer that he finally gained his release for a short while before he died.

The books written by the Krays weren't the only examples of literature about their criminal career. Countless books have been written about their criminal enterprise, as well as being written by various members of both members of The Firm and by members of rival gangs.

Maybe the most famous book about the Krays is The Profession of Violence by John Pearson. Different from most of the books written about the Krays, it was written by a man who was actually contacted by the twins and asked to write their biography.

Well researched and endorsed by the twins, The Profession of Violence was so well received and not written just to cash in that it ended up being made into a very successful film.

Krays-related media has almost become a sub-genre of the crime genre itself with most books about gangsters being linked to the Kray twins in some fashion. Their name being linked to a book automatically gives it credibility, especially for some of the unknown villains who didn't make enough money from their criminal career, and so try to supplement their pension with tall tales and sometimes outright lies.

It's not just the world of literature that the Krays' legacy and influence has extended to, the music industry has also used their name in its output, although not as shamelessly as the publishing houses of the world. Artists as diverse as Blur, The Libertines, Morrissey and Ray Davies of The Kinks have all referenced the Krays in their song lyrics.

Of course, those artists mentioned didn't need a rub from the Kray twins in order to sell records. They were either already established or had enough talent that they would make it there in the end regardless. One such band who didn't fall under this category was a band named Renegade Soundwave, whose first single was entitled Kray Twins. Although they did have roots in the East End, it was still an attempt at cashing in on the notoriety of the Krays, and while they did achieve some degree of success, they never managed the longevity of the other artists who used the Krays in their songs.

While the Krays were never officially named in the titles of any plays, they were used as the basis for two plays in the 1970s. Alpha, Alpha in 1972 was the first play that was loosely based on the lives of the Kray twins. It never achieved mainstream success, although it perhaps would have if the title had explicitly mentioned them by name.

The second play to use Ronnie and Reggie as a basis for their story was England, England; a musical which was first debuted in 1977. Similarly to Alpha, Alpha it never achieved mainstream success. It received higher praise than Alpha, Alpha; partly due to having Bob

Hoskins in the lead role providing some star power. Just like Alpha, Alpha we'll never know if a specific mention of Ronnie and Reggie would have helped it to achieve more success, given how it helped book sales.

Not only are the Krays still a huge influence on literature, they play a big role in the film world. Before mentioning the numerous films about the Krays, their influence and legacy is telling in almost every British gangster film - Guy Ritchie in particular being very influenced by the lifestyle, image and mystique of the Kray twins. Lock, Stock and Two Smoking Barrels and Snatch both borrow their imagery heavily from the way the Krays dressed and carried themselves. As well as the imagery, Ritchie himself has admitted to being heavily influenced by the 1970 film Performance.

Performance is an important film for cinema in general. Guy Ritchie isn't the only director who is influenced by it. Quentin Tarrantino wears the influence heavily on his sleeve in Reservoir Dogs and Pulp Fiction. While it may seem at first the film isn't directly influenced by the Krays, the main character in the film is a bisexual gangster from the East End of London. While that similarity may seem enough to show that it is at least partly based on the life of the Krays, there is more to prove it.

The lead role of Chas was played by the actor James Fox. While he was researching for the role, to ensure he played it to the best of his ability he met with Ronnie in prison to gain an insight into how he thought and why he acted the way that he did. Performance wears its influence very obviously, the Krays legacy extends even to films not directly related to them.

The first actual film about the life of the Krays was the 1990 film entitled simply The Krays. The film starred brothers Gary and Martin Kemp, of the new romantic band Spandau Ballet, as the Kray twins. While the film does cover the violent and ruthless aspects of the twins' lives, it focused more on their interactions with their Mother and with each other. The screenplay, written by Philip Ridley, utilized some creative storytelling, particularly the dialogue of their Mother which reportedly infuriated the real Ronnie and Reggie.

They were not happy about the way their Mother cursed in the film. They said that she never cursed in her life. They also felt that Martin and Gary Kemp were not intimidating enough to play them. They felt that they 'weren't scary enough', especially given their past in a new romantic band. The critics, however, didn't feel the same. It won numerous awards and was nominated for a number of others. While the critics felt the film was of a good quality, it didn't resonate as well with the public. The film never received a wide release at cinemas and only grossed $2 million at the box office.

It was another twenty five years until another Kray film was released: The Rise of the Krays. It didn't go down the usual route of glamorizing the life of Ronnie and Reggie. Instead, it portrayed them in a very realistic light. It showed their cruelty, their evil nature, and ultimately the unstable criminals that they actually were. While many people thought that The Rise of The Krays was quickly put together to capitalize on the high budget mainstream movie, Legend starring Tom Hardy, it was actually in production before Legend was announced and was simply a coincidence that both films were released in the same year - not a cash in to ride the coattails of the bigger budget film.

Legend was a big budget blockbuster released in 2015. Starring Tom Hardy as both

Ronnie and Reggie Kray, it received mixed reviews upon its release, and was based on the previously mentioned well-received book by John Pearson. There are a lot of inaccuracies in most films that get the big budget treatment, but the most glaring one in this is Reggie's treatment of Frances. While Reggie was undoubtedly a violent man, people who knew him knew that he had great respect for women. He was profoundly against violence against women and the way he was portrayed treating Frances in Legend who certainly have provoked an angry reaction from him if he was still alive.

Not only was it out of Reggie's character to do anything violent to Frances, she insisted many times that Reggie was never physically violent towards her; a claim which was backed up by friends. The film changes the type of abuse portrayed in Pearson's book, from psychological to physical. According to Pearson he regularly threatened to kill her and her family, but never physically harmed her in any way.

The playing down of the part the twins' Mother, Violet played in their lives would not have gone down well either if either of the twins were still around today. Their Mother was an integral part of their lives, someone that they not only loved dearly but looked up to and respected. The first film biopic incurred their wrath after it portrayed their Mother cursing, this one downplaying her influence in their lives would have been greeting with just as much vitriol.

While Legend did well at the British box office, grossing over $20 million, it didn't do so well in America. Maybe this speaks volumes for their influence in England, as opposed to overseas. In England, they were, are and probably always will be a big deal, whereas in America they fall under the radar because they can't compete with American anti-heroes in terms of violence and infamy.

The final film biopic to date about the Krays is The Fall of the Krays in 2016. A low budget sequel to The Rise of the Krays from 2015. It was met with almost universally bad reviews. It was a film served no real purpose, especially with the previous year having had two films about the Kray twins released. While the first film was an honest attempt at making a biopic about the pair, this film was considered to be nothing more than a shameless cash-in.

Conclusion

That fact speaks volumes about the lasting legacy of the Kray twins. Although they were vicious, brutal and cruel killers, Ronnie and Reggie Kray both had charm and charisma that captivated people. Their story still interests people, seventeen years after the death of Reggie Kray, and almost fifty years after they were jailed. The Kray twins have a big appeal, especially in England.

While their effect on the East End of London doesn't physically bear their name, it is their legacy. London will never be the same because of Ronnie and Reggie. Their biggest success though, is that their name is still seen as a draw by the entertainment industry. Even after their death, Ronnie and Reggie still have the capability to make money. It's just that these days, it's for other people and a lot less people get hurt. Ronnie and Reggie Kray may well have been criminals, but their names are something that very few can forget.

43009123R00143

Made in the USA
Lexington, KY
22 June 2019